KILLING
THE IMPOSTER
GOD

JB JOSSEY-BASS

KILLING THE IMPOSTER GOD

PHILIP PULLMAN'S
SPIRITUAL IMAGINATION IN
His Dark Materials

Donna Freitas and Jason King

BICENTENNIAL

1807
WILEY
2007

BICENTENNIAL

John Wiley & Sons, Inc.

Published by Jossey-Bass
A Wiley Imprint
989 Market Street, San Francisco, CA 94103-1741   www.josseybass.com

Wiley Bicentennial logo: Richard J. Pacifico

Jossey-Bass books and products are available through most bookstores. To contact Jossey-Bass
directly call our Customer Care Department within the U.S. at 800-956-7739, outside the U.S.
at 317-572-3986, or fax 317-572-4002.

Jossey-Bass also publishes its books in a variety of electronic formats. Some content that appears in print may not be available in electronic books.

Library of Congress Cataloging-in-Publication Data
Freitas, Donna.
Killing the imposter God: Philip Pullman's spiritual imagination in his dark materials /
Donna Freitas and Jason King.
    p. cm.
Includes bibliographical references and index.
  ISBN-13: 978-0-7879-8237-9 (pbk.)
  1. Pullman, Philip, 1946- His dark materials. 2. Pullman, Philip, 1946--Criticism and interpre-
tation. 3. Fantasy fiction, English—History and criticism. 4. Young adult fiction, English—
History and criticism. I. King, Jason, 1971- II. Title.

PR6066.U44Z66 2007
823'.914—dc22   2007023338

Printed in the United States of America
FIRST EDITION
PB Printing   10 9 8 7 6 5 4 3 2

CONTENTS

Conclusion: *Building the Republic of Heaven*   161

To Kelly and Julianna

INTRODUCTION
A Theologian in Spite of Himself

Those that hate goodness are sometimes nearer than those
that know nothing at all about it and think they have
it already.

C. S. LEWIS, *THE GREAT DIVORCE*[1]

Although I call myself an atheist, I am a Church of England
atheist, and a 1662 Book of Common Prayer atheist,
because that's the tradition I was brought up in and I cannot escape those early influences.

PHILIP PULLMAN (FROM LAURA MILLER, "FAR FROM NARNIA:
PHILIP PULLMAN'S SECULAR FANTASY FOR CHILDREN."[2]

In the very first line of *His Dark Materials*, Philip Pullman gives
us what may be his most spectacular invention: the dæmon,
or, more specifically, his heroine Lyra Belacqua's dæmon, Pantalaimon (Pan, for short). Best understood as something like
"soul-creatures," dæmons manifest themselves outside the
body, making each human and that human's animal-formed
"soul" (both changing infinitely and whimsically until the
onset of puberty) an interdependent pair. From there we are
propelled into Lyra's adventures in a parallel world's Oxford,

similar enough to our reality to recognize, yet distinct in ways that immediately alert us to the breadth of Pullman's ability to re-imagine worlds and everything in them. We follow Lyra to the North, accompanied by the proud, sea-faring Gyptians and Iorek Byrnison, a very human-like armored bear, as Lyra tries valiantly to thwart the intentions of her beautiful but evil mother, Mrs. Coulter, to perform "intercision": the permanent separation of children from their dæmons.

Most dramatically of all, we journey with Lyra over a bridge into another world, Citagàzze—the place where she will meet Will, who is destined to be her best friend and first love. Will is to be the bearer of perhaps the second most imaginative invention in the trilogy: the subtle knife—a dagger that cuts between worlds. Given all this, it is not surprising that Pullman's fantastic retelling of Milton's *Paradise Lost* has quickly captured the imagination and intellect of thoughtful adults and critics as well.

After finishing the trilogy, Gregory Maguire, author of *Wicked* and *Son of a Witch* and many other novels, marveled:

> I might reread the complete saga at once. I want to organize all these worlds in my mind. I want to test the implications of the theology to make sure that they are supported by the contortions of the plot. I trust that many readers, young and old, are going to be left with magnificent questions. The big ones. And why not? That's what books are for.[3]

Pullman's trilogy, indeed, leaves us with magnificent questions, and there is little doubt that *His Dark Materials* is a rare literary achievement. Through Lyra and Will, we are drawn into a multilayered universe of grand adventures, parallel worlds, and mythical creatures, leading many to wonder what world they would visit if wielding the subtle knife, what sort of dæmons would comfort and enliven them, and, of course, whether Will and Lyra will somehow manage, not only to save the world but to transform it into something better. We believe the complexity of Pullman's characters, universe, and inventions, taken together, is enough to warrant a deeper look at the trilogy by its devoted readers.[4]

Among the wider public, Philip Pullman's *His Dark Materials* is already considered a classic, receiving both astounding media attention and critical acclaim.[5] In a contest called "The Big Read," held by the British Broadcasting Corporation (BBC) in 2003 as a "celebration of the magic of reading," Pullman's trilogy ranked third, behind only Tolkein's *Lord of the Rings* and Jane Austen's *Pride and Prejudice*.[6] Clive Anderson, the narrator of a BBC special about *His Dark Materials,* praised the trilogy as "the most dangerous, terrifying, breathtaking book you'll ever read," a story that is far more "than a kid's fantasy."[7] William Flesch of *The Boston Globe* called it "thrilling—in some ways perhaps the most electrifying piece of literature of the past 20 years."[8] And in a frequently cited review in *The New York Review of Books,* novelist and critic Michael Chabon had this to say about Pullman's invention of the dæmon:

> The Goddess of writers was smiling upon Pullman
> on the day he came up with the idea for dæmons. . . .
> My eight-year-old daughter expressed what I imagine
> is a near-universal response of readers, young and
> old, to *His Dark Materials* (and probably the ultimate

secret of the stories' success): "I wonder what kind of dæmon I would have!"⁹

His Dark Materials is rightly praised as endlessly complex, wildly adventurous, and layered throughout with Big Questions about good and evil, beauty and brutality, meaning and despair—questions that are equally beguiling to both children and adults, albeit with different levels of understanding.[10] It is a tribute to Pullman's fertile imagination that so many thinkers from so many different fields—children's literature, adult literature, psychology, psychoanalysis, physics, and biology—have taken up the task of exploring its significance.[11] And as our world reels from the impact of war, anxieties about terrorism, religious fundamentalisms of all sorts, and the political and cultural imperialism of the West, Pullman provides us with a rich, epic tale that eerily resonates with these contemporary challenges.

But he also provides us with a story replete with *theological* questions.

A UNIVERSE WITHOUT GOD?

Across the three books of the trilogy—*The Golden Compass* (Knopf, 1995), *The Subtle Knife* (Knopf, 1997), and *The Amber Spyglass* (Knopf, 2000; books noted in text as GC, SK, and AS, respectively)—the loves, betrayals, deceptions, and loyalties of Pullman's worlds take place under the arc of a sacred canopy, where spiritual beings are plenty and the divine is immanent. But instead of making room only for the lost, the different, and the good, this religious umbrella also provides protection for lies, corruption, and all manner of evil, including a quasi-divine "Authority," who is a dictator in the truest and most vile sense. Reflecting Pullman's public statements about his own atheistic position, at first glance it would seem that through *His Dark Materials*, Pullman provides us a window into a universe *without* God.

In *The Amber Spyglass*, Balthamos, one of two angels who hope to join forces with Lord Asriel (Lyra's father) by delivering to him the subtle knife, evokes the evil deity who rules the many worlds of *His Dark Materials* by using names for God that are familiar to the Judeo-Christian tradition: "The Authority, God, the Creator, the Lord, Yahweh, El, Adonai, the King, the Father, the Almighty," Balthamos lists (AS, 31). This "Authority" turns out not to be a god at all but instead an *imposter*—an angel masquerading as God. This despot gets his comeuppance when Pullman orchestrates his now infamous death toward the end of *The Amber Spyglass*. This particular scene has sparked great controversy among religious readers and a thinly veiled glee among the secular. It has also shined a spotlight on the author who, in its glow, has trumpeted his atheism to interviewers far and wide. About the religious significance of this particular moment, Maguire wonders: "Is this a book about the death of God or about the defeat of an institutionalized authority? Can there be temptation in a world in which sin has lost its meaning? Is there a creator of all things?" And we question further: When is religion a means toward salvation, and when is it a tool of destruction? Is there room for the divine in the ostensibly atheistic universe of *His Dark Materials*?

Then there is perhaps our biggest query of all: Is *His Dark Materials* really about killing God?

In an interview posted on the author's Web site, when asked directly whether *His Dark Materials* is "against organized religion" and, if so, whether this means that Pullman does not believe in God, he responds:

> I don't know whether there's a God or not. Nobody does, no matter what they say. I think it's perfectly possible to explain how the universe came about without bringing God into it, but I don't know everything, and there may well be a God somewhere, hiding away.
>
> Actually, if he is keeping out of sight, it's because he's ashamed of his followers and all the cruelty and ignorance they're responsible for promoting in his name. If I were him, I'd want nothing to do with them.[12]

Is *His Dark Materials* Pullman's exploration of what a universe looks like "without bringing God into it," or is it more likely that somewhere in its many worlds, "there may well be a God somewhere, hiding away"? As longtime lovers of *His Dark Materials,* his books do not seem to us as if they "are about killing God" or depicting a universe where God is "keeping out of sight" and "wants nothing to do with his followers."[13] Lyra and Will's incredible universe appears to have a divine force that desires, desperately so, to be in communion with its creation. In fact, we believe Pullman's work echoes the concerns of liberation theologians—people whose primary concern is that the divine be an empowering, life-changing energy for humanity and the earth—so much so that his trilogy can be read as a religious classic. It is different in nature, certainly, from Lewis's *Chronicles* but not less significant in its rich parallels with the Jewish and Christian traditions Pullman himself so publicly adjures.

A Public Champion for Atheism

Europe, of course, has become famously secular over the last century, with Great Britain—Pullman's home country—a particularly bright star in the firmament of what sociologist Peter Berger has termed "Eurosecularity." Much attention has been devoted to exploring Europeans' "godlessness," as well as the related mystification of Europeans concerning the religious devotion demonstrated by Americans.[14] So the fact that Pullman self-identifies as an atheist is not surprising. Yet his ability to broadcast this atheism is unique. Although many public figures—politicians, writers, and journalists alike— surely share Pullman's anti-religious leanings, few share the stature that comes from penning a best-selling series of novels that dare to kill off God. And the reach of his pulpit is ever-expanding, now that New Line Cinema has brought *His Dark Materials* to the screen.[15]

But Pullman's atheism was not always so front and center, nor was it always so explicit. In 1998, Pullman admits, in an article about C. S. Lewis's popularity called "The Dark Side of Narnia," that he detests "supernaturalism," but this is a tame suggestion compared to his current fervor and openness about his disdain for religion and God.[16] As early as 1996, when Pullman first achieved real public note after winning the Carnegie Medal for *The Golden Compass*, his acceptance speech vaguely alludes to a distaste for the "moral education" campaign for public schools waged by the Archbishop of Canterbury and the Secretary of State for Education and Training occurring at the time of his award, explaining that, "We don't need lists of rights and wrongs, tables of do's and don'ts: we need books, time, and silence. Thou shalt not is soon forgotten, but Once upon a time lasts forever."[17]

But this commentary is also relatively mild, as compared to the explosion of conversation about Pullman's atheism that erupted *only* after the publication of *The Amber Spyglass*—the final book of the trilogy, which includes the most controversial material in the trilogy: the death scene of the Authority.

Since the release of *The Amber Spyglass* in 2000 and its subsequent, dramatic increase of press for the trilogy, Pullman has lost no further time molding himself into what *The New Yorker* writer Laura Miller describes as "one of England's most outspoken atheists."[18] One interviewer from *The Times* in London claimed that Pullman's atheism has become "legendary" and that this ideology grounds and shapes all his writing about humanity.[19] In 2000, Kate Kellaway of *The Observer* described Pullman as "an atheist with a mission," who "describes science as the 'most successful achievement of the human race,'" implying that *His Dark Materials* is, indeed, part of "Pullman's atheist's mission" and that he sees religion and science as diametrically opposed.[20] In much the same way that children blindly follow the alluring yet evil Mrs. Coulter in *The Golden Compass*—trading their safety for her beauty and a steaming cup of hot chocolate—journalists and critics alike have accepted on faith, as it were, that Pullman's personal attitudes about atheism are inextricably linked to *His Dark Materials,* and he has done little to dissuade them.

Pullman has also championed his atheism in a plethora of interviews and articles about the trilogy. Of theology, religion, and God, Pullman has said many things, including: "I don't profess any religion; I don't think it's possible that there is a God; I have the greatest difficulty in understanding what is meant by the words 'spiritual' or 'spirituality.'"[21] Moreover, through the mouth of the witch queen Ruta Skadi in *The Subtle Knife,* he writes that "every church is the same: control, destroy, obliterate every good feeling"[22] (SK, 50). In an interview with journalist Susan Roberts, Pullman comments:

> I'm caught between the words "atheistic" and "agnostic." I've got no evidence whatever for believing in a God. But I know that all the things I do know are very small compared with the things that I don't know. So maybe there is a God out there. All I know is that if there is, he hasn't shown himself on earth. But going further than that, I would say that those people who claim that they do know that there is a God have found this claim of theirs the most wonderful excuse for behaving extremely badly. So belief in a God does not seem to me to result automatically in behaving very well.[23]

Though here Pullman might give God an inch, his disdain for religion is clear: even if there is a God, no one has evidence to support this claim, and people who believe in God use this belief to do terrible things. Pullman also made quite a splash for designing a course for British schools called "Why Atheism?" with his colleague Michael Rosen. This curriculum, for children eleven years and older, features "disbelieving" students talking openly about the reasons they do not believe in God, and former Christians, Muslims, Jehovah's Witnesses, and Hindus explaining why they rejected their respective religions.[24]

Particularly in the wake of the terrorist attacks on 9/11 and in light of the religiously motivated wars and genocides that are ongoing across the world, the idea that belief in God sparks bad behavior (to put it mildly) is a fair assessment. But it is not the *only* fair assessment about religious belief, and Pullman's frequent, personal equation of God (whether a false version or not) and the church with evil, betrays his biggest bias as a thinker, and, we worry, may now inevitably cloud his readers' ability to encounter what we see as a fantastically sophisticated understanding of the divine lurking throughout the trilogy. Pullman cares supremely about the power of the human imagination and the role that freedom of interpretation plays in shaping it. Yet when it comes to religion and God, Pullman seems to forget about his commitment to what he calls a "democracy of reading."[25] Pullman is now so forthright about his atheism (not least on his own Web site)—it is now a rare article about his fiction that *does not* reference it in one form or another—that he has made it virtually impossible for readers to engage this trilogy without his personal views about God perched somewhere in their minds.[26] Even positive reviewers note that Pullman, who criticized Lewis for preaching in his *Chronicles,* "falls prey to that same bad habit himself . . . [and] . . . to facilitate his preaching, he breaks many of the rules of fantasy-writing in this third volume [*The Amber Spyglass*]."[27]

Despite all this, we wonder: Did Pullman initially *intend* his trilogy as an atheist's manifesto? And even if he did, must we always read it as such?[28] Or can we still approach his work, as many do, with C. S. Lewis's *The Chronicles of Narnia*, as if it has nothing to do with its author's theology?

STAGING THE DEATH
OF AN IMPOSTER GOD

In 1966, in one of its most controversial issues, *Time* magazine ran an all-black cover adorned only with the question, "Is God Dead?" The occasion was the sudden popularity of "Death-of-God" theology, which aimed, not so much to exterminate as to resuscitate God. "At its worst, the image that the [medieval] church gave of God was that of a wonder worker who explained the world's mysteries and seemed to have somewhat more interest in punishing men than rewarding them," *Time* noted. The editors then featured so-called Christian Atheists—theologians such as Harvard's Harvey Cox and Gabriel Vahanian of Syracuse University, who believed that the contemporary church was suffocating under the impress of an outdated view of the divine. The aim of most of these Death-of-God theologians—and they *were* theologians—was not to promote atheism but to save Christianity.

Pullman's *His Dark Materials* would have fit very well into this Death-of-God movement, which sought to shock Christians out of the juvenilia of believing in a Superman-type false God who rules from the clouds and into a more worldly vision of the divine, suited to the realities of science and the truths of the Enlightenment.[29] In many ways, the trilogy itself acts as a kind of obituary for God, just as death notices for divinity began appearing in American newspapers in the 1960s:

Atlanta, GA., Nov. 9: "God, creator of the universe, principal deity of the world's Jews, ultimate reality of Christians, and most eminent of all divinities, died late yesterday during major surgery undertaken to correct a massive diminishing influence. Reaction from the world's great and from the man in the street was uniformly incredulous. . . ."

From Independence, MO, former President Harry S. Truman, who received the news in his Kansas City barbershop, said "I'm always sorry to hear somebody is dead. It's a damn shame."[30]

But Pullman's funeral rites are for a very particular sort of image of God—the tyrannical God of the Middle Ages—and, unlike his predecessors in the Death-of-God movement, his atheism is by no means in the service of faith. The God whom Pullman kills in *His Dark Materials* is, by the author's own admission, a false God, reminiscent of the medieval church with its pious pomp and unjust inquisitions. But was not this God already long dead among many believers? Isn't there room for God still after this particular imposter God is extinguished?

We believe the answer is yes and find support for this response throughout *His Dark Materials*. Or, to put it another way, we find some of the most eloquent testimony against Pullman-the-atheist in Pullman-the-writer; we read this trilogy as a religious classic of considerable sophistication. Even as Pullman is killing off his medieval imposter God, he raises up for his readers a divinity fit for our age—one compatible at once with science, popular spirituality, and contemporary theology—the very sort of divinity that the Death-of-God theologians of the 1960s were seeking and that the feminist and liberation theologians of the 1970s and beyond found. We interpret the trilogy as a call to let go, once and for all, of the childish, medieval view of God. And though Pullman the writer may, indeed, stage the death of an imposter God in *The Amber Spyglass,* we feel he resurrects a far more sophisticated divinity throughout the trilogy.

THE LOGISTICAL PARTICULARS

In the upcoming chapters, we follow the trilogy closely, trying in each character's motives and actions to find the "true" nature of God that Pullman's story reveals to us. We approach *His Dark Materials* on its own terms rather than reading it through Pullman's repeated public proclamations of his atheism, though we do not keep Pullman's work isolated entirely from Pullman-the-atheist thinker. Although we respect Pullman's self-identity as an atheist, we do question how useful *His Dark Materials* is as a tract for same. At least when it comes to proselytizing, this trilogy is closer to Lewis's *Chronicles* than Pullman himself may want to admit.

More broadly, we hope to put one particular contemporary vision of the Christian God, as articulated by liberation and feminist theologians both Protestant and Catholic, into conversation with *His Dark Materials.* Perhaps somewhat ironically, we see Pullman's trilogy as a powerful example of how a self-professed atheist has created what could be read as a contemporary Christian classic—one that fits boldly within conversation in this particular "branch" of theological conversation.

Pullman's work fits into this conversation, we think, because he is consistent with liberation theology on several points:

1. Liberation theologians evaluate the Christian God against the critical lens of whether this God serves to free people from oppression based on gender, race, economics, or other social factors, rather than leave them disenfranchised and disempowered through God's rule.

2. Liberation theologians read the Bible in ways that are conducive to this kind of freeing, even if the reading is not traditional. These thinkers focus on human experience here and now, in *this* world, pointing to God's work to free people from slavery in Egypt and Jesus as a model for changing the political and social structures of the world, creating a kind of "heaven on earth."

3. Liberation theologians focus on relationships, on the interconnectedness of friends, families, and even those we consider our enemies—often giving their theology a *panentheistic* slant, which not only understands God as central to all relationships but understands creation and the divine as so intimately connected that, though God may indeed "transcend" God's creation, the universe is also God's body.

4. Feminist theology is usually regarded as a particular type of liberation theology, with the issue of gender as its guiding concern.

Our book is divided into three parts, with three chapters in each; at the end of the book is a Conclusion ("Building the Republic of Heaven"), followed by a section titled "Plot Summaries," where we give readers a refresher course in the plot of each novel, as well as character descriptions and definitions of important objects like Lyra's alethiometer.

In Part One, we explore Pullman's beliefs about God, starting with the final scenes of *The Amber Spyglass* and its unheroic death of an aging and withered God.

Part Two turns from theology to ethics, exploring Pullman's understanding of good and evil and examining his emphasis on freedom and compassion as interrelated values.

Finally, most religions teach some concept of divinity, a code of ethics, and a way of liberation or salvation. The last of these characteristics is meant to address the seemingly inevitable fact that something is awry with each of us and unsatisfactory about the universe. So Part Three explores Pullman's notion of salvation: How do Will, Lyra, and Mary help others to become free, thoughtful, conscious, and kind? Chapters in this last section look at how people's spirits are saved, how their bodily existence is saved, and, finally, how God is saved as well.

One last note: What we love so much about *His Dark Materials*—and we do love these books—is the very fact that whenever we begin to try to pin down the books' significance, it becomes ever more elusive.[31] Pullman himself says that, ideally, "a storyteller should be invisible, as far as [he's] concerned; and the best way to be sure of that is to make the story itself so interesting that the teller just disappears." Pullman, of course, has forgotten to follow his own advice, at least when it comes to the question of God.[32] But we happily and passionately take up the task of turning Pullman's universe on its head by sampling of this forbidden fruit. We hope that the other scholars, writers, and readers of Pullman, who have begun a wildly diverse conversation about these novels, will join us in leaping fences and crossing boundaries, as we all seek to explore the depths of this fascinating trilogy. From our small corner of the universe, we present Pullman's work as embodying a sophisticated theology and so make the atheist Philip Pullman a theologian in spite of himself.

Yes, but what kind of theologian?

KILLING
THE IMPOSTER
GOD

But when Zarathustra was alone, he spoke thus to his heart:
"Could it be possible? This old saint in the forest has not
yet heard any of this, that God is dead!"

NIETZSCHE, *Thus Spoke Zarathustra: A Book for None and All* [1]

PART ONE

The Dark Matter of God

In *Women and the Word,* feminist theologian Sandra Schneiders ascribes our contemporary inability to think outside the box when it comes to the divine as one of the great failures of the Western imagination. There is no reason for us to limit our theological options, Schneiders urges, to voting for or against the ancient Patriarch in the sky, particularly when contemporary theologians have made available to us myriad images of the divine—personal and abstract, gendered and ungendered, literal and metaphorical.[2]

For German liberation theologian Dorothee Söelle, our imagination fails us when, because of our fixation on the patriarchal God of Judaism and Christianity, we are unable to see the divine immanent among us, particularly in the poorest of the poor, in the downtrodden and the needy, and in those around us who are experiencing despair. For Söelle, it is in the oppressed that we come face to face with the divine, for the divine lives among us and dwells within us, and not only in pain but in love and even lovemaking, too. When one body truly loves another, Söelle observes, the divine comes into the world in community.[3] Finally, Grace Jantzen and many other European feminists hear the reverberations of the divine among the voiceless, empowering them to find a voice—to speak, to write, and, most of all, to desire a divine fitting for this experience. It is in and through the ecstasy of bodies that we come to see the divine in ourselves and invite divinity into our communities.[4]

In the three chapters that follow, we apply this feminist and liberationist thinking about the Christian God—thinking that sees God not as an enemy of freedom, creativity, love, and ecstasy but as their friend—to show how the trilogy is actually a tribute to this particular vision of the divine.

Chapter One explores the possibility that Pullman is not really waging a war on God. His complaint instead is with a certain kind of authoritarianism, one that is, indeed, found within some interpretations of the divine but is absent from many others. Chapter Two shows how *His Dark Materials* offers a complex yet fairly common vision of God and proposes that Pullman's decision to wage war against an imposter God and a corrupt church highlights feminist and liberation theologians' particular concerns with human freedom and liberation from oppression. Finally, Chapter Three explores how Pullman's triune understanding of humanity as body, soul, and ghost follows neatly from the God we see evident throughout the trilogy.

He is an old white man with a long white beard . . .
sitting on a golden throne in heaven,
surrounded by clouds. . . .
At His feet is a heavenly host of angels in white
robes, with harps. (Once the harps were swords and
the heavenly hosts were the army of God defending
His heavenly palace.) . . . God loves the world and
its creatures. But He sometimes gets angry and
unleashes His wrath on the sinners. . . .
If we do not follow His will, we will be punished
by being sent to hell to be burned in eternal flames,
along with Satan.

CAROL CHRIST ON THE "OLD WHITE MAN" GOD IN
TRADITIONAL CHRISTIANITY; FROM *She Who Changes*[1]

CHAPTER

I

CONFUSING GOD
WITH "AUTHORITY"

In a move reminiscent of Friedrich Nietzsche's prophet Zarathustra, who proclaims the death of God to anyone who will listen, Pullman "kills" God in one of the climactic moments of *The Amber Spyglass*. Pullman's false God—the first angel that lords over the parallel worlds of Lyra and Will's universe—is a paper-thin, ailing fake, who expires with a gasp of relief into the molecules of the atmosphere. But his presence (and the Authority is unmistakably a *he*) lords over the trilogy. Any writer who plays so fast and loose with God—describing him as a pretender and then killing him off—knows he is making a statement. But surely part of that statement is that God is to be taken seriously.[2]

OF THE DEVIL'S PARTY?

Of course, given Pullman's choice to follow Milton's *Paradise Lost* in retelling the story of the Fall, God is going to have some part to play. Waging war on God (or the gods) is a story that stretches nearly as far back as stories themselves. As long

7

as there have been stories about gods, at least, there have been storytellers who challenge the authority of the gods and seek to overthrow them. Prometheus's theft of fire from and subsequent punishment by the ancient Greek gods is but one of many examples of the pervasiveness of war on the reigning deities. So Pullman's trilogy is not remarkable in this regard. Yet Pullman offers us an intriguing twist on this oft-told tale, because in this case God is not only defeated but his destruction is a blessing for the universe. Satan is not the villain for Pullman. God is the villain, making explicit in this version of *Paradise Lost* what many (Pullman included) have long suspected about Milton—that he was "of the Devil's party without knowing it."

Yet, as we say in the Introduction, *His Dark Materials* is far from godless; we think it is a contemporary Christian classic. And although Pullman's greatest inspiration for *His Dark Materials* may have been Milton's *Paradise Lost,* echoes of the death of God in Nietzsche's *Thus Spoke Zarathustra* ring throughout the trilogy. Zarathustra's proclamation of God's death by no means makes Nietzsche an atheist. The same is true of Pullman, whose concerns, like those of Nietzsche himself, closely track those of Christian liberation theologians. Exploring their similarities will help determine whether Pullman (at least as the writer of *His Dark Materials*) is really the atheist he makes himself out to be or a Christian theologian of a very contemporary sort.

THE FRAGILITY OF "AUTHORITY"

When Nietzsche put "God is dead" on the lips of his cryptic prophet Zarathustra, he sealed his own fate as an atheist, even among those who have never read this nineteenth-century

German philosopher. But the three words Nietzsche is most remembered for uttering are some of the most misunderstood in the history of philosophy. With a little theological exploration, it is all too easy to see why Nietzsche is not really an atheist—like the Death-of-God theologians of the 1960s—but is rejecting an outmoded Christian understanding of the divine.

The God who dies in *Thus Spoke Zarathustra* is very similar to the Authority who "dissolves into nothing"—"a mystery dissolving into mystery" (AS, 411)—in *His Dark Materials*. The divine figure that Zarathustra pronounces dead is someone who kills imagination, creativity, and self-development—a god who paralyzes human will, buries us in fears of sin, and otherwise keeps us from really living. Feminist theologian Sallie McFague offers a description of a similarly authoritarian divinity whom Pullman calls "the old one" (AS, 410) and that she terms the monarchical God:

> God as king is in his kingdom—which is not of this earth—and we remain in another place, far from his dwelling. In this picture God is worldless and the world is Godless: the world is empty of God's presence for it is too lowly to be the royal abode. Time and space are not filled with God: the eons of human and geological time stretch as a yawning void back into the recesses, empty of the divine presence; the places loved and noted on our earth, as well as the unfathomable space of the universe, are not the house of God. Whatever one does for the world is not finally important in this model, for its ruler does not inhabit it as his primary residence, and his subjects are well advised not to become too involved in it

either. The king's power extends over the entire universe, of course, but his being does not: he relates to it externally, he is not part of it but essentially different from it and apart from it.[3]

For Nietzsche, and for many contemporary feminist and liberation theologians like McFague, this kind of remote-ruler God is not really worthy of the title. His objective is keeping his subjects under his thumb, in endless submission to his authority. This kind of blindly narcissistic authority, however, is also very fragile; it lasts only as long as one's subjects agree to their subordination. As soon as an individual becomes aware of having been made party to the laws and rule of another, that person tends to rebel, that is, to pursue, as the German philosopher Hegel put it, "the fulfillment of his own immediate will and natural impulses," quite apart from the hold of the larger authority.[4]

This same predicament, of course, bedevils Pullman's God figure—the Authority—whose rule is made fragile by a rising awareness among a few individuals that they can choose not to follow his whims. The Authority, so old, senile, and impossibly withered by the time Lord Asriel mounts armies against his rule, has only his Regent—the second most powerful angel, Metatron—to defend his last shreds of power and maintain his kingdom in the clouds. It is difficult not to wonder: Has the Authority been so weakened by maintaining this long charade that his once robust effort to guard his rule has sapped him of all energy and will? And though the Authority is oft-mentioned by the time readers reach *The Amber Spyglass*, he is spoken of in name only. By the end of the trilogy, when we finally meet this famously feared figure, it becomes questionable whether he still holds enough power *to still be an authority*. We can't help but think that he is entirely "spent" and must have ceded the job of holding his subjects in check to Metatron long ago.

Readers first learn of Pullman's Authority figure in *The Subtle Knife*, during a conversation between Lord Asriel's servant Thorold and the witch Serafina Pekkala. "But you know about our God?" Thorold asks the witch queen—"the God of the Church, the one they call the Authority?" Thorold knows that the witches have other gods—that the so-called God of the Church is not the only god worshipped in the universe. "Well Lord Asriel has never found hisself at ease with the doctrines of the Church, so to speak," Thorold continues, explaining his theories concerning Lord Asriel's disappearance:

> It's my belief he turned away from a rebellion against the Church, not because the Church was too strong, but because it was too weak to be worth the fighting. . . . I think he's a-waging a higher war than that. I think he's aiming a rebellion against the highest power of all. He's gone a-searching for the dwelling place of the Authority Himself, and he's a-going to destroy him. (SK, 45–46)

This passage alludes not only to the epic battle between Satan and God in *Paradise Lost* but also to the biblical book of Revelation, more specifically to the Ruler who rules from a throne. As with Carol Christ's old man who lives high in the clouds and Sallie McFague's God-king, whose dwelling is somewhere far from earth, Pullman's Authority lords over the worlds from a hidden domain—the Clouded Mountain, where he is not vulnerable to an attack by those who resist his reign, where he can maintain an aura of mystery around him and perhaps even hide his tired state.

Yet little else is said of this God of the Church, who will soon see his reign collapse, until Pullman reveals the truth behind this imposter God in *The Amber Spyglass*. After Will asks the angel Balthamos whether the Authority really is God, Balthamos responds with a definitive no:

> [The Authority] was never the creator. He was an angel like ourselves—the first angel, true, the most powerful, but he was formed of Dust as we are. . . . The first angels condensed out of Dust, and the Authority was first of all. He told those who came after him that he had created them, but it was a lie. . . . And the Authority still reigns in the Kingdom. (AS, 30–31)

The Authority's reign has hung for thousands of years on a single, fragile circumstance: although the Authority was an angel, he was not known as one. Because of the simple fact that he preceded all the others, the Authority was able to deceive his fellow angels (and, eventually, almost every intelligent creature in the universe) into believing that he was their creator. The Authority was able, by the force of this lie, to coerce them into submission and the whims of his desires for order, and the ways not only of life but also of death—at least at first. With the help of other angels, the Authority set up the church in Lyra's world (where it still holds great power) and others, including Will's (where by the time of the trilogy, its existence is barely evident), to communicate his deception to all sentient beings, using force and violence to secure obedience from those unconvinced by the lies.

So for thousands of years the Authority got away with portraying himself as the god that created the universe and all the "lesser" creatures in it, promising to watch that creation, protecting creatures in it in return for their trust and obedience. But even once we meet Will in his Oxford, it becomes clear that science has begun to trump any effective church rule, and in Citagàzze the church rule seems absent altogether, implying that in at least some worlds, the Authority retains only a whisper of power, if any at all.

In other words, by the time of the trilogy, the Authority is poised to "Fall."

THE "FALL" OF "AUTHORITY" OR THE DEATH OF GOD?

The Authority's original deception from which all other deceptions flow hangs on a single thread, which becomes frayed as the truth begins to leak out. The Authority's original lie is gradually unmasked in Lyra's world over the course of the trilogy, and as the truth begins to spread throughout his kingdom, it becomes evident that the true Fall in *His Dark Materials* is the fall of the Authority himself. As evidence of the Authority's lies builds and chatter about his true nature spreads, he grows quiet and moves into seclusion. The Clouded Mountain, once a throne of great power, increasingly becomes a hiding place for this would-be God—a movable fortress that allows the Authority to run away as his power is challenged. Of the Clouded Mountain and its growing occlusion, Balthamos explains:

It's sometimes called the Chariot. It's not fixed, you see; it moves from place to place. Wherever it goes, there is the heart of the Kingdom, his citadel, his palace. When the Authority was young, it wasn't surrounded by clouds, but as time passed, he gathered them around him more and more thickly. No one has seen the summit for thousands of years. (AS, 28)

By the time Lord Asriel goes to battle against "God" in *The Amber Spyglass,* the Dust particles that constitute the Authority's being are so tenuously linked that he is protected by a seemingly impervious, hollow glass globe.

A strikingly similar tired and grandfatherly God appears in Nietzsche's *Thus Spoke Zarathustra*—one who in his youth was a vengeful ruler but is now weakened—and emasculated— by age and made weary by humanity. As Nietzsche's pope character explains:

He was a concealed god, addicted to secrecy. . . . When he was young, this god out of the Orient, he was harsh and vengeful and he built himself a hell to amuse his favorites. Eventually, however, he became old and soft and mellow and pitying, more like a grandfather than a father, but most like a shaky old grandmother. Then he sat in his nook by the hearth, wilted, grieving over his weak legs, weary of the world, weary of willing, and one day he choked on his all-too-great pity.[5]

The Herculean effort required to maintain such a grand deception for thousands of years reduces Pullman's diminished Authority and Nietzsche's ailing God alike to virtual nothingness. Exhausted, these "Authorities" finally become as vulnerable to death as their subjects.

In a key battle scene in *The Amber Spyglass,* Metatron moves the Authority away from the heart of the fighting. Metatron does so on the sly, using only a few guards and a miniscule caravan. Lord Asriel's forces do not notice this retreat, but some ugly vulture-like creatures looking for war spoils to pick at—the cliff-ghasts—do. When Will and Lyra stumble upon the Authority, he appears to be simply another angel, though a frighteningly aged one. The cliff-ghasts have already killed all his guards and are trying to break the glass globe protecting him. But Will scares the ghasts away with the subtle knife. Afterwards Will and Lyra stare into the globe and have pity on the diminished and demented being known as the Authority.

> "Oh, Will, he's still alive! But—the poor thing. . . ."
>
> Will saw her hands pressing against the crystal, trying to reach in to the angel and comfort him; because he was so old, and he was terrified, crying like a baby and cowering away in the lowest corner.
>
> "He must be so old—I've never seen anyone suffering like that—oh, Will, can't we let him out?"
>
> Will cut through the crystal in one movement to help the angel out. Demented and powerless, the aged being could only weep and mumble in fear and pain and misery, and he shrank away from what seemed like another threat.
>
> "It's all right," Will said "We can help you hide, at least. Come on, we won't hurt you."

The shaking hand seized his and feebly held on. The old one was uttering a wordless growing whimper that went on and on, and grinding his teeth, and compulsively plucking at himself with his free hand; but as Lyra reached in, too, to help him out, he tried to smile, and to bow, and his ancient eyes deep in their wrinkles blinked at her in innocent wonder.

Between them they helped the ancient of days out of his crystal cell; it wasn't hard, for he was light as paper and he would have followed them anywhere, having no will of his own, and responding to simple kindness like a flower to the sun. But in the open air there was nothing to stop the wind from damaging him, and to their dismay his form began to loosen and dissolve. Only a few moments later he had vanished completely, and their last impression was of those eyes, blinking in wonder, and the sigh of the most profound and exhausted relief. (AS, 410–411)

Little more than a ghost himself at this point, the Authority returns in this moment to the universe—Dust to Dust—the way ghosts emerging from the Land of the Dead dissolve into the atmosphere. The æsahættr, the God-destroyer (the other name for Will's subtle knife), performs this task, not out of malice but out of love. Using the hands of two children, Pullman has scripted for his readers what is now one of the most controversial moments of *His Dark Materials*—a scene that has led some to label him "the most dangerous author in Britain."[6]

PULLMAN: A THEIST AFTER ALL?

Unlike Pullman, who in this climactic moment banishes the divine from the universe, Nietzsche allows himself to imagine, through the voice of Zarathustra, the sort of god who would be to his liking:

> I would believe only in a god who could dance. And when I saw my devil I found him serious, thorough, profound and solemn: it was the spirit of gravity— through him all things fall.
>
> Not by wrath does one kill, but by laughter. Come, let us kill the spirit of gravity!
>
> I have learned to walk: ever since, I let myself run. I have learned to fly: ever since, I do not want to be pushed before moving along.
>
> Now I am light, now I fly, now I see myself beneath myself, now a god dances through me.
>
> Thus spoke Zarathustra.[7]

For Nietzsche, the idea that somehow one omnipotent God is the sole source of creativity in the universe sucks the life out of humanity by disassociating all value from humanity and placing it elsewhere (with God). The God of traditional Christianity—external, static, and wholly other—acts like a chain on humanity, restricting every person's "will to power" (to use another famous Nietzchean phrase) or, to put it in language common to liberation theologians, their will *to be empowered.* For Nietzsche, it is not every understanding of God but this *particular* understanding of God that must pass away so that humanity may be empowered and its creative potential liberated. The "superman" (or "overman," depending on the translation) is "capable of doing more than just experiencing value as a separate object." He (or she) can encounter the world as if "spirit and nature are no longer opposed to one another," and "is capable of giving birth to an alternative human project," explains one Nietzschean interpreter.[8]

When Nietzsche wrote at the end of the nineteenth century, there was little theology available that would cotton to his tastes or to his understanding of God. When an old magician speaks to Zarathustra of the angst brought on by the loss of god, Nietzsche reveals his sense that the death of even this traditional God is a tragedy for humanity. Yet it is a necessary tragedy, since it opens up space for a new sense of the divine to emerge in the old God's place. Nietzsche's magician comments quite prophetically: "Of all of you, who like me, are suffering of *the great nausea,* for whom the old god has died, and for whom no new god lies as yet in cradles and swaddling clothes."[9]

True, a god dies in *Thus Spoke Zarathustra.* But in that same text the seeds of a "new god" are sown—an alternative vision of the divine that makes room for becoming, imagination, creativity, and all those other things that Nietzsche valued. Today that "new god" can be seen in a wide variety of alternative theologies that were themselves unimaginable in Nietzsche's time: the panentheism of Alfred North Whitehead that envisions the evolution of the world as the evolution of God, the liberation theologies of Gutiérrez and Boff and others that re-frame Christianity to be a source of empowerment and not oppression, and even (though Nietzsche was no feminist) the feminist theologies of Catherine Keller and Sallie

McFague, which take panentheism and transform it into a theology that seeks justice for all creatures.[10]

His Dark Materials, of course, came into the world more than a century after Nietzsche pronounced God dead and prophesied the emergence of a new divine better suited to humanity's creative and imaginative capacities. Pullman wrote this trilogy during a theological era when alternative visions of the divine abound, so it is hard to understand how Pullman overlooked all these available alternatives and why he seems unable—or at least unwilling—to consider his own alternative divinity in the trilogy. Pullman has by no means killed off God in general. He has killed off only one under-standing of God—*God-as-tyrant*—and an oddly antiquated and unimaginative one at that. Pullman has done away with the malicious, lying, controlling, manipulating being in charge of his universe in order to put an end to unjust cruelty and domination. But he says nothing about the many other gods that are worshiped across the world's religions or about more sophisticated understandings of the Christian God.

On the surface, Pullman looks like a protest atheist. Protest atheism is a category in the study of religion used to name a person or tradition that explicitly rejects a particular notion of God—the trinitarian God of Christianity, for exam-ple, or a Jewish God who allows the Holocaust to occur.[11] Zen Buddhists are told, "If you meet the Buddha, kill the Bud-dha."[12] In other words, do not elevate anything into the ulti-mate authority. Do not let anything—even God—interfere with your quest for enlightenment. When asked whether there was a god, Siddhartha, the historical Buddha, refused to answer. If you are shot with an arrow, he elaborated, you do not bother with a series of philosophical questions about who shot the arrow or at what angle or speed. Instead, you pull out the arrow and reduce your suffering. In this life then, one should not be concerned with metaphysical speculation about gods or the afterlife; one should be concerned with ending suffering here and now. The Buddha does not say there is no god. He simply says that existing notions of god are not relevant to his project of reducing suffering.[13]

Although Pullman seems to fit the heading of "protest atheist," he diverges from this category in one crucial way. Protest atheists do not reject one god in order to offer up another in its place. And that is precisely what Pullman does in *His Dark Materials*. Pullman clearly rejects a particular notion of God in *The Amber Spyglass*, but he goes on to offer an alternative interpretation of the divine. The name of this divinity is *Dust*, and Pullman gives over its study to people in Lyra's world, whom he refers to as "experimental theologians."

Be at one with the dust of the earth.

This is primal union. . . . This therefore is the

highest state of man.

LAO TZU, *TAO TE CHING*, #56[1]

CHAPTER

2

A GOD MADE
OF DUST

It might seem odd that out of all the substances he could
have made precious in *His Dark Materials,* Pullman chose
Dust—that most ordinary stuff that settles on our furniture
and underneath our feet. Many interpret the line from Genesis that tells us we are made from dust as an indication of
our nothingness in comparison with God. We are, essentially,
dirt. But by calling the most precious stuff in *His Dark Materials* Dust, Pullman turns on its head this typical interpretation of human nature. Just as Pullman turns Lyra—his
representation of Eve from Genesis—from a scapegoat into a
heroine, he radically re-values Dust itself. In Pullman's universe, Dust, as Mary Malone and Serafina Pekkala and others
who gaze through the amber spyglass are able to see, is exquisitely beautiful, even divine.

WHY DUST?

In many sacred texts of the world's religious traditions—the
Bible, the Torah, the Koran, and the Tao Te Ching, among
others—dust is the substance from which humanity is made.

In Genesis, God says to Adam after the Fall: "In the sweat of thy face shalt thou eat bread, till thou return unto the ground; for out of it wast thou taken: for dust thou art, and unto dust shalt thou return" (Genesis 3:19). And in the Koran, as with Adam, we learn that God made Jesus from dust: "Truly, the likeness of Jesus, in God's sight, is as Adam's likeness; He created him of dust, then said He unto him, 'Be,' and he was" (the Koran 3:59). It follows in these traditions that because humanity is good, dust is also good. And so it is in Pullman's trilogy as well.

In *His Dark Materials,* all life, as Lyra and Will know it, rests on Dust; their fates rest on its fate, as without Dust all intelligent life in the universe would fall into a kind of living death. Dust is a force that appears more and more as the trilogy progresses, and in each instance we learn a little more about its nature. It is what powers Lyra's beloved alethiometer—the beautiful "golden compass" that answers Lyra's questions, that looks strikingly similar to "a large watch or a small clock: a thick disk of gold and crystal" (GC, 73), with "hands pointing to places around the dial, but instead of the hours or the points of the compass, there were several little pictures, each of them painted with extraordinary precision, as if on ivory with the finest and slenderest sable brush" (GC, 78)—a treasure Lyra guards close on her person at all times. Dust is what speaks through Mary Malone's Cave, the Oxford scientist from Will's world who runs the Dark Matter Research Unit, and who, together with the help of Lyra, determines that the mysterious dark matter she investigates—these "Shadow particles" that help all things in the universe to "hang together and not fly apart," and that "make gravity work" (SK, 86–87)—is not only the same as Lyra's Dust, but that Dust, Shadow particles, dark matter—whatever one calls it—are actually "particles of consciousness" (SK, 88). And not only is Dust both conscious and consciousness, but Dust is what angels are made of, as "angels are creatures of shadow matter," also "what we have called spirit" (SK, 249), which means that the Authority is *also* one being among many made of Dust.

We learn the most important lesson about the nature of Dust and its many names and manifestations, though, when Mary Malone adjusts her Cave—the machine she has constructed to communicate with Shadows—and the Shadows start to literally talk back. Ask us a question, they say, and after Mary gets over her initial shock, she does just that. When the Shadows respond, she learns that Dust is the ultimate, unifying, and animating principle of the universe:

Are you Shadows?	YES.
Are you the same as Lyra's Dust?	YES.
And is that dark matter?	YES.
Dark matter is conscious?	EVIDENTLY. (SK, 248)

After the Shadows urge Mary to ask more and more questions, we find out the most interesting news of all about the nature of Dust:

| The mind that's answering these questions isn't human, is it? | NO. BUT HUMANS HAVE ALWAYS KNOWN US. |

Us? There's more than one of you?	UNCOUNTABLE BILLIONS.
But what are you?	ANGELS . . .
Angels are creatures of Shadow matter? Of Dust?	STRUCTURES. COMPLEXIF-ICATIONS. YES.
And shadow matter is what we have called spirit?	FROM WHAT WE ARE, SPIRIT; FROM WHAT WE DO, MATTER. MATTER AND SPIRIT ARE ONE. (SK, 248-249)

So Dust is the "spirit" of human beings and all matter but also the "form" of angels. Throughout the trilogy angels are said to mimic Dust in possessing consciousness, attention, desire, creativity, and imagination. At one point Pullman's readers learn that the beings called Angels look longingly on humans because of their materiality—a reality made so evident in the intense love relationship between Baruch and Balthamos (the two angels who so long to unite with each other in any and every way possible) that "Balthamos felt the death of Baruch the moment it happened," so much so that it was as if "half his heart had been extinguished" (AS, 83). Dust not only loves itself, but it loves matter. Dust seeks embodiment. Dust enlivens bodies with consciousness, and when bodies become animated with the stuff of angels, these enlivened bodies in return seek knowledge—all kinds of knowledge, including the knowledge of other bodies and of the love and desire that the body expresses for other bodies.

Once we are able to set aside Pullman's personal professions of atheism, it is not difficult to see how Dust takes on many qualities that are typically associated with the divine. Dust existed since the beginning. It always tells the truth, whether through the alethiometer or through Mary Malone's Cave. Dust is the source of all creation: of matter, spirit, angels, dæmons, humans, and every creature imaginable. It generates consciousness in people, infusing bodies with souls and spirits and with an unquenchable desire for freedom. But more than simply generating consciousness and freedom in sentient beings, it urges these beings to save both on behalf of others. It imbues Lyra with the grace that enables her to read the alethiometer; it urges Lyra to stay with Will, and it directs Mary Malone out of her world so that she might help Will and Lyra. And in *The Amber Spyglass* we learn that Dust has yet another name: Wisdom—a name for God that many feminists have devoted much energy to exploring.[2] In the Wisdom literature in Hebrew scripture, God is referred to in the feminine. In other words, Wisdom—*Sofia* in Greek, and the Holy Spirit, the third person of the Trinity in Christianity—is a *she*.[3] In *His Dark Materials,* wisdom is also a she—a she-angel who, because of her defiance of the Authority, "has had to work in secret, whispering her words, moving like a spy through the humble places of the world while the courts and palaces are occupied by her enemies" (AS, 479).

Although Dust has many qualities classically associated with Western notions of God, Pullman has infused Dust with many other qualities that are *not* typical. Commenting on the difficulty of seeing God in something other than a classic understanding of the divine, feminist philosopher Grace Jantzen explains:

> One of the areas of greatest internal disagreements [in Western theology] is between those who insist that God as the divine Absolute must be eternal and thus timeless and changeless and those who argue that such changelessness, far from being an attribute of perfection, is actually a characteristic only of dead things or of abstract thought rather than of anything living.[4]

Toward the end of *The Subtle Knife* and throughout *The Amber Spyglass*, we learn that Dust falls into the latter category. Far from static, it depends upon human consciousness and action to continue to exist. As the angel Xaphania explains to Will and Lyra at the end of *The Amber Spyglass*, "Dust is not a constant. There's not a fixed quantity that has always been the same. Conscious beings make Dust—they renew it all the time, by thinking and feeling and reflecting, by gaining wisdom and passing it on" (AS, 491). Without people, Dust can disappear. And it waxes and wanes, depending on what happens in the universe. The fact that Dust is "spirit" does not mean that it is not also physical; it is spiritual-matter. In fact, every conscious being is made of spiritual-matter. To be conscious *is to be spiritual*. Although Dust differentiates itself into different beings, it is not fundamentally divided. Put simply, the world and everything in it is Dust. So while Dust may be divine, it is miles apart from the classic understanding of God as all-powerful, all-knowing, and immutable, wholly other and independent from all creation.

In Pullman's universe, there is a mutuality between Dust and all creatures, an inherent connection between Dust and the universe itself. In other words, Dust seeks relationships. In fact, it *requires* them for its own survival. It wants not simply to be *but to be loved*; it *needs* to be loved. And in needing love and being loved, in its desire to be held as dear by its creatures as Baruch and Balthamos find each other so precious that one would die on behalf of the other, it also becomes *vulnerable*—able to be destroyed, or at least endangered, as a result. In fact, we encounter a number of concrete ways that Dust is threatened throughout the trilogy. Each time Will uses the subtle knife to cut a door into another world, it creates "wounds . . . in nature" (AS, 403), causing a "leak" through which Dust spills out of the universe, diminishing its presence in creation. The terrible specters, those horrifying creatures that "gorge" themselves on humans' souls, their dæmons (SK, 130), are actually feeding on Dust, endangering Dust in yet another way, by sucking away this enlivening force from the world's intelligent creatures. The abyss that lay along the edge of the Land of the Dead—the place, the prison camp, that "great chasm in the underworld" (AS, 429) to which the Authority has banished everyone's ghosts after death—also acts as a black hole, sucking Dust downward and out of the worlds at a frightening pace. And eventually we learn that, without the efforts of intelligent beings, without their love and subsequent desires to act on this love of Dust, to preserve it, Dust will eventually die off until it is lost to the worlds forever—a topic to which we come back to for the entirety of Chapter Nine, "Love's Divine Sacrifice."

This is perhaps the quality of Dust that may make some readers decide it is decidedly *un*god-like, and utterly distinct from any Christian notion of God—its vulnerability, the fact that it can be endangered, and, as a result, that like the created, it is itself in need of salvation. But as Jantzen testifies, the aloof and unchanging God of traditional Christianity is not the only option. In fact, what we regard as Pullman's vision of the divine precisely tracks a lesser known (at least beyond the halls of academe) but nonetheless powerful understanding of God that emerged early in the twentieth century and is widespread among Christian theologians today.

UNDERSTANDING WHY DUST IS DIVINE

More specifically, Pullman's understanding of Dust bears key resemblances to a vision of the divine championed by process philosophers, liberation theologians, and feminist theologians. Upon reflection, we see that Pullman is no atheist. He is instead a *panentheist*. *Pan* means "all" and *theos* means "God," so, while *pantheism* literally means "all is God," *panentheism* means "all *in* God" and reflects the notion that God retains a kind of transcendent quality. (And please note: the word *pandemonium*, which is so reminiscent of Lyra's Pantalaimon, translates as "place of all demons" and first appears in Milton's *Paradise Lost*.)[5] Pantheists believe that everything is, at its root, one, so there is nothing that is *not* God. Therefore, they are also referred to as monists (who affirm that "all is one"). The problem with pantheism though, explains feminist theologian Carol Christ, is that it "has difficulty asserting that individuals other than Goddess/God exist."[6] So many theologians turn to pan*en*theism, which understands that God has an independent nature; yet these theorists believe that the universe itself is God in the process of becoming: *God evolving*.

One of the earliest thinkers to affirm a panentheistic notion of the divine was Alfred North Whitehead. Originally a mathematician at Trinity College in Cambridge, Whitehead became the founder of process philosophy or "process metaphysics." When he started to think about God, he concluded that one ultimately cannot separate God from human beings and the world they inhabit. All is connected. God and human beings emerged together and grow together. Each one develops with and depends upon the other, and so they are in process together.[7]

Although Whitehead's views are at odds with traditional Christianity, which holds that God has a different nature from the world and human beings, several Christian thinkers have found panentheism helpful in explaining some of Christianity's key beliefs and values. Both liberation and feminist theologians have often drawn on panentheism to underscore the importance of relationships among people and the intimacy between God and humanity.[8] David Tracy, a professor of religion at the University of Chicago, has argued that panentheism, specifically, describes the God of the Bible more accurately than the remote authoritarian figure.[9] Understood through this lens, God has real emotions, responds to people, and is affected by people's experiences. Such a God becomes manifest through the material world. The Jesuit paleontologist Pierre Teilhard de Chardin, who shared many of the sympathies of Whitehead's process philosophy, argued that a panentheistic notion of God is scientific, since it better reflects the evolutionary reality of the universe. After all, the God of panentheism is about *Becoming* and not simply about *Being*.[10]

Pullman's views are in line with those of panentheistic theologians in a number of ways. His concept of divinity clearly resides within the universe, and beings in that universe are infused with the stuff of the divine. Yet individuality and freedom are core values in the worlds where Lyra and Will live, and Dust clearly has a will of its own. So *His Dark Materials* replaces the classic God of Western monotheism—a God separated from matter and the human race, a God who dominates both time and space—with a God that is *part of* time, matter, and space, yet also retains a degree of independence. God is among us and is affected by people—God is interdependent with us—yet without taking away anyone's freedom. This degree of independence, or *transcendence,* Mary Malone discovers when she first attempts to communicate directly with Shadows through the Cave and realizes they have a consciousness all their own.

According to Carol Christ, a panentheistic understanding of the divine also offers a vision of God that affirms creation, bodies, and all the processes of life characteristic of both creatures and the earth itself. For Christ, panentheism

> clearly understands that men as well as women are embodied, related, and interconnected in the web of life. . . . [It] offers a holistic understanding of the world in which change and embodiment and interdependence are affirmed for all individuals— women, men, animals, cells, the smallest particles of an atom, and Goddess/God. . . . also [affirming] that all individuals are free and creative . . . [reminding] us that all bodies—male as well as female, nonhuman as well as human—are part of the divine body and thus can function as images of divinity.[11]

In panentheism, mind and body and consciousness and beings are not understood as separate from each other but as an inseparable continuum, reciprocally related to one another. In fact, they are so intimately related that one literally cannot be without the other. As Christ explains:

> Panentheism means that the world is "in"
> Goddess/God . . . because Goddess/God
> sympathetically feels the feelings of every creature.
> Insofar as the world is also understood to be the
> body of Goddess/God, panentheism can also be said
> to mean that Goddess/God is "in" the world, is felt
> by and included in every creature.[12] *Can anybody tell me what the ' just said?*

Finally, the divine power that resides in a panentheistic God "keeps the creative process of the universe from deteriorating into chaos," much the way Dust keeps intelligent life alive in the universe of *His Dark Materials*. At the same time, "panentheism asserts that divine power is always the power of persuasion, not coercion, power with, not power over."[13] Just as becoming conscious or becoming "knowledgeable" must be freely chosen by beings in the worlds of Lyra and Will, so individuals in a panentheistic universe are *empowered* by a God intimate with their world and even their bodies, rather than being ruled by a remote divinity supremely detached from the joys and despairs of embodied life.

After the death of the Authority and his Regent, Metatron, the true power in Pullman's universe is revealed to be Dust—a power devoted to truth, freedom, consciousness, and creativity; a power that says yes to embodiment and to living a meaningful life; a power compatible with the desires of Lyra, Will, Lord Asriel, and Will's father, the explorer and shaman

Again the method is always to oppose a nice caring, feminist divinity with the "straw man" (or God) whom no one would worship: right) "mind would think the sort of Jesus in St. Paul and still think that God is a remote detached divinity."

John Parry, to build a certain version of the "Republic of Heaven" on earth—a topic we come back to in greater detail in Part Three. The fate of this power is not foreordained, however, as Dust's continued existence is inextricably bound with the fate of all creatures. Pullman, despite his personal professions of atheism, has, indeed, created within *His Dark Materials* a universe replete with the divine.

You know the Church—the Catholic Church that I
used to belong to—wouldn't use the word dæmon,
but St. Paul talks about spirit and soul and body.
So the idea of three parts in human nature
isn't so strange.

MARY MALONE TO WILL AND LYRA (AS, 439)

3

WE ARE, EACH OF US,

DIVINE

At the start of *The Golden Compass,* Lyra and her dæmon, Pantalaimon, are sneaking into the Retiring Room at Jordan College. At this point in Lyra's life and nascent adventures, Pan (who is a moth in this scene) can and does take on different shapes: dolphin, wildcat, mouse, owl, wolverine, and so on. Adults' dæmons cannot do this, because at the onset of puberty they settle into one and only one form. Servants' dæmons tend to settle into submissive creatures such as dogs that "trot obediently" after them as they do their masters (GC, 5); the powerful Lord Asriel's is a majestic and fearsome snow leopard, Stelmaria, and the seductive Mrs. Coulter's is a golden monkey, whose fur is so lush that it's almost irresistible to the touch, despite taboos against one human touching another's dæmon.

WHAT IS A DÆMON?

Dæmons are intimately connected to individual people. If a person dies, so does the person's dæmon, vanishing immediately from sight with the human's last breath. If a person's dæmon dies, that person's death cannot be far off, and whatever life he or she has left without the dæmon barely merits the term. Though humans are not supposed to touch another person's dæmon, dæmons can touch one another, and they do quite often, at times playfully, but at others as a show of force or to create fear, as when Pantalaimon and Mrs. Coulter's golden monkey get into a vicious fight, and he is "wrestling, biting scratching at Pantalaimon, who was flickering through so many changes of form it was hard to see him, and fighting back: stinging, lashing, tearing" (GC, 297). Each dæmon is attached, though not in a literal sense, to a particular person and cannot go very far, usually only a few yards, from that person without causing some stress at short distances and excruciating, heart-rending pain at long distances. Witches are the main exception to this rule; witches' dæmons are not restricted to their respective witches' locations. This odd unfettering of a witch and her dæmon is what sets the witches apart and makes people in Lyra's world suspicious of them.

This idea of the dæmon is not only one of the most distinctive aspects of *His Dark Materials* but also one of the main reasons why this work is considered fantasy. Pullman, however, insists that he could care less about fantasy and is only curious about reality:

> I'm not writing about elves and goblins and so on.
> I couldn't care a fig for any of those things. Human
> beings are my subject matter. And although this
> story [*His Dark Materials*] has fantasy elements, I
> think at the core of it is something which is as
> realistic as I could possibly make it. . . .[1]

For Pullman, dæmons are not some clever device for literary effect. Pullman uses them to highlight his trilogy's representation of human nature.

As Lyra is traveling north with the Gyptians—the nomadic boat-people led by patriarchs John Faa and Farder Coram— she enters into a conversation with a seaman about dæmons. He reminisces about his childhood fear that his dæmon would settle as a porpoise and thereby trap him on a boat at sea. Lyra says that she never wants her dæmon to settle; she never wants to grow up. But the seaman kindly tells her about the benefits of a dæmon settling into one form.

> Take old Belisaria. She's a seagull, and that means I'm a kind of seagull too. I'm not grand and splendid nor beautiful, but I'm a tough old thing and I can survive anywhere and always find a bit of food and company. That's worth knowing, that is. And when your dæmon settles, you'll know the sort of person you are.
>
> But suppose your dæmon settles in a shape you don't like?
>
> Well, then, you're discontented, en't you? There's plenty of folk as'd like to have a lion as a dæmon and they end up with a poodle. And till they learn to be satisfied with what they are, they're going to be fretful about it. Waste of feeling, that is. (GS, 167–168)

The form a dæmon finally settles on reveals the essence of the person. Dæmons capture both the blunt and the subtle characteristics of their human, revealing their strengths and weakness: Mrs. Coulter's golden monkey is beautiful to look upon but vicious and conniving underneath, just as she is; the dæmon of John Faa, "lord of the western gyptians," is a crow, representing his "air of strength and authority" (GC, 114), and Sir Charles Latrom, the man who tries to trick Will into giving him the subtle knife by stealing Lyra's alethiometer, has a snake for a dæmon, symbolic of his evil nature and self-serving intentions.

Pullman, in short, seems to be using dæmons as something akin to individuals' souls. A person who is severed from her or his dæmon through *intercision*—the shockingly evil, experimental process overseen by Mrs. Coulter in the North at the lab, Bolvangar—becomes less than human. When Lyra finds Tony Makarios severed from his dæmon Ratter, Tony is only really a half-child. Cut away from his beloved life-long companion, he clutches a dead fish in a confused attempt to comfort himself, muttering softly, incomprehensibly, almost too weak to despair from the permanent loss of his beloved life-long companion. A person whose dæmon has been removed is also called a partial person—a zombie or an undead, as with the specters that feed on the souls of adults in Citagàzze. People without dæmons may be able to survive, but theirs is a subhuman existence without meaning or purpose: a soulless life.

Pullman's notion of the soul differs, of course, from typical assumptions about souls. Most contemporary Western views of the soul owe much to Plato, who argued that the soul is eternal; it existed before the body and will exist after it. In the *Phaedo*, Plato's recounting of Socrates' death, Socrates explains how none of the things that affect human beings are able to affect the soul. Death, age, and sickness destroy the body, but they do not destroy the soul. That is because the soul is immaterial; it does not rely on a body.[2] Yet Pullman's dæmons share more in common with Aristotle's understanding of the soul. Dæmons are physical beings that exist only in union with a specific human being. According to Aristotle, souls cannot be separated from the body except by death. Souls animate bodies, making us uniquely human, intelligent creatures. Once the body dies, the soul dies. There is no place apart from the material world for a soul to escape to. The soul is part of this world rather than eternity, existing only in conjunction with a particular body, in this particular time and space.[3]

Officially, the Christian notion of the soul is much more similar to Plato's version, since Christians believe that the soul exists independently of the body after death. But Christians typically do not believe, as Plato did, in the existence of the soul before conception or in its reincarnation after death. Christians also distinguish themselves from Plato (who disdained the body and saw the soul's separation from it as ideal) by viewing the person as an indivisible amalgamation of body and soul. God made human beings as bodies and souls. The division at death into souls separated from bodies is not what God intended, so at the end of time, when all of creation is remade, new bodies will rise from graves and individual souls will be reunited with their perfected bodies.[4] Although this notion of the soul has always been the official teaching, Christianity often seems to encourage a sort of gnosticism about the body's relationship to the soul. Gnosticism affirms (among other things) that the soul is good, perfect, and holy, and the body is evil, imperfect, and corrupt.

There are many forms of gnosticism, but each version usually has a myth about how souls suffer the misfortune of getting trapped in bodies.[5] Gnostics would reject Pullman's notion of the dæmon. By making the dæmon both material and spiritual—by embodying the soul, in other words—Pullman is, from a gnostic perspective, polluting the only pure aspect of human existence.

Do Bodies Matter?

The story of Mary Malone—the Oxford scientist who decides to take a leap of faith, not only to trust Lyra but to leave her lab and world behind to journey through a window into an unfamiliar land—is, in one respect, quite simple. She was once a nun, she tells Lyra and Will toward the end of *The Amber Spyglass*—not one who was cloistered or wore a habit, however, but a physicist. She presented a well-received paper at a conference, went out to dinner, remembered a time of falling in love, and decided that she did not want to live without this feeling. So she left her religious vocation, she explains to them, as they sit outside her house admiring the starry night among the *mulefa*—the strange, intelligent wheel-creatures Mary has befriended, and whose culture's survival depends on saving Dust.

Every turn of Mary's story is contingent upon some aspect of her physical existence. As a nun who is also a scientist, Mary studies the physical world, and this preoccupation is what draws her to the physics conference in Lisbon, where she has this revelation that changes the course of her future. She leaves her room after her presentation to have dinner and drinks with some friends and thoroughly enjoys the sardines, wine, warm air, and music that permeate the evening. She talks with one of the men at the table, wants him to think that she is pretty, and flirts with him. She enjoys these physical experiences, and this bodily pleasure makes her question what good being a sister and forsaking these things really does for others. Absolutely nothing, she decides, as she reaches for the sweet marzipan on the table, whose taste sparks a sudden flood of memories from when Mary was twelve. A boy had fed her a piece of marzipan, and when he touched her lips with it, she fell in love with him. Eventually they kissed, but he soon moved away and she became a nun. When she tastes the marzipan anew, this time she realizes that she wants not only to study the physical world but, above all, she desires the embodied experience of falling in love again. So she leaves the church.

This story turns out to be crucial to the plot of *His Dark Materials* because, in describing to Will and Lyra the physicality of falling in love, she gives them a way to understand their mutual affections. Later, when Will and Lyra are left alone, Lyra turns to Will and places a small red fruit on his lips and he eats it. This act has obvious echoes to the Garden of Eden story from Genesis, but it also replays Mary Malone's earlier encounter with love and marzipan. Through their exchange of fruit and affection, Will and Lyra communicate both their attraction to one another and its corresponding joy. Immediately, they start to kiss and, thanks to Mary's story, they are able to communicate their love for each other, not just in words but through their bodies.

This praise and respect for the body and its pleasures permeates Pullman's trilogy. Food, drink, music, touch, and taste all bring great joys to existence. These are intimately connected to what it means to be not only an intelligent creature but an embodied one. In Pullman's universe, it is only through bodies that people come to know the truth about themselves and others. Mary learns that she likes the physical world and that her life of religious denial is not true to herself. Lyra and Will learn not only how they feel about one another but also how to act on these feelings. In short, without the experience of the body, people lose a key aspect of life, without which they cannot truly know themselves or their world.

Pullman's emphasis on the body sets him at odds with many Eastern traditions, like Hinduism, which sees the body as external to the real person, which is spiritual. In the *Bhagavad Gita,* Krishna, an incarnation of the god Vishnu, counsels the warrior Arjuna to do his duty in the war set before him and not to fret about killing. Death only destroys the body but not the Atman, the Hindu version of the soul, which after death will be reincarnated in a new body. "As a man discards worn-out clothes to put on new and different ones, so the embodied self discards its worn-out bodies to take on other new ones."[6]

Pullman's insistence on the body's value situates him much closer to the Christian tradition, which affirms that God made the physical world and all the bodies in it, and not only judged it all to be good but united with it in the person of Jesus. From this divinely embodied perspective, humanity is to be honored and respected. The core caveat of these Western traditions is that, while the body is important—a major constituent of the self—it is not necessarily the most important aspect of existence. As Jesus' death on the cross demonstrates, physical life must sometimes be sacrificed for the spiritual life—a reality we encounter at the very end of *His Dark Materials,* when Will and Lyra must say goodbye forever in order to save Dust, sacrificing their future as lovers for something they decide is a higher purpose (and that we discuss in depth in Chapter Nine). Although Pullman largely resists this ascetic urge to sacrifice the body to the spirit, he also recognizes that the body is not everything; in fact, we will find that his entire trilogy is, in effect, a tribute to this ideal. Through the voices and actions of his characters, Pullman recognizes that there are other dimensions to the human person. The dæmon is one. But there is also the spirit.

What About the Spirit?

In *The Golden Compass,* Lyra sets out to rescue her friend and partner-in-crime Roger, who had been taken by the Gobblers—those feared child-stealers employed by Mrs. Coulter in an effort to find participants for her experiments with intercision. She manages to rescue Roger, only to hand him over unwittingly to Lord Asriel, who kills him in a brutal scene at the end of this first installment of the trilogy. Lyra is almost broken by the realization that she betrayed a friend whom she meant to save, but with his death, she also witnesses the astounding power of the dæmon.

Later, in *The Amber Spyglass,* Mrs. Coulter has drugged Lyra to keep her asleep. During this sleep, Lyra converses with Roger, now trapped in the underworld, the Land of the Dead. Roger begs her to help him and worries that Lyra will mistakenly believe that their conversation is only a dream. When Will rescues Lyra, she recalls Roger's pleas and what seems like his terrible fate, as well as her betrayal of him, so she commits herself to his rescue. Will agrees to accompany her, but neither Will nor Lyra realizes that they have committed themselves to a perilous journey into the underworld, a horrifying place populated only by ghosts.

When Lyra asks the alethiometer how to help Roger, she is told that she and Will must go to this Land of the Dead, an answer that puzzles them both. What is there to rescue in the Land of the Dead? "[D]æmons fade away when we die . . . and our bodies, well, they just stay in the ground and decay, don't they?" (AS, 166). In this way, Will and Lyra realize that there must be a third part to human beings, a part that is neither body nor soul, a part that can think about the other parts. "And that's the ghost," Lyra concludes, and she and Will set out to rescue Roger's ghost.

Ghosts, or spirits—an uncountable number of them—are what Will and Lyra encounter once they arrive in the Land of the Dead. These beings are transparent reflections of their once-living bodies—a state that sends most of them into despair. Spirits cannot touch one another. Color fades from them. They can speak only in whispers. All passion and desire seems to have drained out of them so that they appear to be entirely powerless creatures. When the two children enter the Land of the Dead, the extraordinary fullness of their persons carries more power and authority than all the millions of ghosts combined. The ghosts are drawn to their color and their warmth. In fact, Will and Lyra feel as if their body heat is being stolen by the ghosts' cold hands. Stripped as these ghosts are of body and soul, they are no longer really persons but merely echoes of their former selves. Seeing Lyra and Will, so vibrant in their embodiment, reminds the ghosts of what they used to be and what they long to have again.

These once-human beings as ghosts are left with their spirits, however, and we know that the spirit is vital for any person to be fully alive. The spirit is what makes a person conscious and free; people need the spirit to "think about [their] body" and "think about [their] dæmon" (AS, 166). Without it, they become zombie-like. The soul might embody a person's essence, and the body might enable communication with others, but without the spirit, without the ability to reflect on and understand these other aspects of the human person, body and soul alike become inert lumps. If the soul constitutes the person's drive for self-identity, and the body is how the person experiences the world, then spirit is consciousness, self-awareness, and the ground for all true freedom.

People Made of Dust

Pullman's three-dimensional notion of the human being is deeply Christian. When Mary Malone affirms Lyra and Will's belief in this three-part structure of the human person, she specifically cites St. Paul—and a vision of our being that echoes the Christian tradition's trinitarian notion of God. Mary says, "You know, the Church—the Catholic Church that I used to belong to—wouldn't use the word dæmon, but St. Paul talks about spirit and soul and body. So the idea of three parts in human nature isn't so strange" (AS, 439).

Like Jews and Muslims, Christians are monotheists, believing in only one God. Unlike Jews and Muslims, however, Christians believe that God is a Trinity. The official formulation of this difficult doctrine is that God is three persons—Father, Son, and Holy Spirit—in one nature. *Person* and *nature* are philosophical terms that carry technical meanings that are more precise than their common usage might indicate. *Person,* in this technical sense of the Trinity, means "a substance of rational nature." Therefore, any being—human, angel, God, or other creature—that has higher reasoning capacity is a person. This essential trait—the kind of animation of being that, in the end, defines our "nature"—is what distinguishes one creature from another and from all other matter. So the Christian definition of the Trinity technically means that in God there are three rational substances that all share whatever it is that makes God, God. The doctrine that says God is three persons in one nature indicates that Christians have three distinct experiences of God—experiences that should not be confused with one another. But these distinct experiences point to one single God.[7]

While the Christian doctrine of the Trinity is intended to articulate a mysterious truth about God, it also implies certain ways in which Christians should behave. Because Christians believe that they are made in the image and likeness of God, and because God is a trinity, which is to say a community of persons, Christians cannot be truly at home in isolation from others. While people are to retain a sense of who they are—just as the Father, the Son, and the Holy Spirit are not to be confused with one another—they can only truly flourish in relationship to other people. If what binds the three persons of the Trinity is love, then people can only reflect the image of God in loving relationships.

Panentheism, which we discussed in the last chapter, tries to capture this reality and more. It readily acknowledges that God is relational, a community even, and that humans are to imitate this interconnectedness. Panentheism not only insists that God is not just a model for human existence; it also affirms that God is inextricably related and bound to human creatures and to creation itself.[8] The essence of a panentheistic God does not stop with three persons but rather extends to all people, respecting their freedom but also making them connected to each other and to the Divine. Pullman's Dust is also a panentheistic notion of the divine, so it should be no surprise that people in Pullman's universe not only imitate Dust but, in fact, *are* Dust.

When Lyra first meets Mary Malone in Will's world, Mary's entire professional life had been devoted to understanding the properties of dark matter, and she is a scholar presiding over the Dark Matter Research Unit. That Unit, however, is in trouble, and Mary is on the verge of losing her job. As we discussed in Chapter Two, her research focuses on an interactive computer called the Cave—a machine designed to help her and her colleague investigate the nature of dark matter; on her door hang handwritten signs saying "R.I.P." and "Director: Lazarus." Mary's project is about to have its funding cut because her research seems to indicate that dark matter is conscious—a conclusion that not only flies in the face of other studies but also appears to move well beyond the bounds of scientific inquiry.

Mary allows Lyra to operate the Cave, and the result is a brilliant display—the best Mary has ever seen. Lyra draws two conclusions from the experience: that dark matter is the same as what she has so far called Dust, and the Dust that operates the alethiometer is also the substance (as the dark matter) that Mary investigates with the Cave. Lyra then tells Mary that she can alter the program in order to speak more directly and clearly with the dark matter. Mary decides to do just that. When she completes this reprogramming in the middle of the night, Mary has a shocking exchange. She is told to flee her world, destroy her research, and play the tempter. Yet in the process Mary also learns something crucial about Dust— about Pullman's vision of the divine: that the dark matter is, in fact, Dust, that Angels are creatures of Dust, and, most important of all, that "matter and spirit are one, from what we are, spirit; from what we do, matter" (SK, 249). Yet these revelations are not only significant to understanding the God of *His Dark Materials* but also the tripartite nature of the human person articulated through the story.

In the universe of *His Dark Materials,* the spirit and the body that make up two-thirds of the person are not easily divisible; both are made of Dust. Spirit is Dust acting in one way ("from what we are"), and matter is Dust acting in another ("from what we do"). In acting to rescue Roger, Lyra opens a doorway out of the Land of the Dead, and, as the dead escape their ghosts, dematerialize and return to Dust. Their spirits, which are Dust, are reabsorbed into a universe also made of Dust. Mary Malone realizes that 30,000 years ago Dust gave rise to consciousness in creatures throughout the multiple worlds.

Lord Asriel shows through photographs that Dust settles on mature, fully conscious adults but not on children. The Angel Xaphania tells Will and Lyra that it is consciousness, or spirit, that generates and preserves Dust. Serafina Pekkala says that without Dust the world would degenerate into a mechanistic entity, devoid of freedom and thought. And even more radical than this conflation of Dust with spirit and consciousness is the conclusion that matter is Dust. Matter (or humans, their bodies) is Dust in action. The body is Dust moving, acting, and interacting. When a person dies and a corpse is laid in the ground, it decays. But the decay enables the matter that made up the person's body—its attendant Dust—to be reabsorbed into the world.

The dæmons are *also* constituted by Dust. When Lee Scoresby, the Texas aeronaut who died covering John Parry's escape, allows his spirit to finally break apart, the thought at the forefront of his mind is that his particles will mingle with those of Hester, his dæmon, whose atoms were waiting for his atoms. Just as the body and spirit are made of Dust and return to Dust, so are dæmons made of and return to Dust. Specters, the vile creatures who inhabit the world of Cittàgazze, suck the souls out of people, leaving them alive but only barely so, less than zombies. When Will and Lyra become old enough to see the specters, the specters go after their dæmons, their souls. It is only later that Will and Lyra realize that the specters "grow by feeding on Dust. . . . And on dæmons. Because Dust and dæmons are sort of similar" (AS, 486). Dæmons are another way that Dust exists in the universe; when a person dies, the Dust that constitutes its dæmon is changed into Dust of a different form and purpose.

Even before Mary knew that dark matter was Dust and that Dust was consciousness, she knew that dark matter was necessary to hold the world together. Her insight was based on a calculation concerning how much matter was needed to hold the universe together, but her insight was truer than she knew. In Pullman's universe, Dust holds everything together. It takes on different forms to become spirit, soul, and body, and to make a person. In this way, Dust becomes matter and the world. Even the angels and the Authority are created and formed out of Dust. Every person and every world, and every spiritual and material aspect of each, is interconnected because they are all made of Dust. So Pullman's panentheism is a deep panentheism, not stopping with a purely spiritual or mystical connection but going all the way down to bodies.

Through *His Dark Materials,* Pullman the writer has retrieved (or perhaps reinvented) a particularly Christian understanding of the divine, the human, and the universe itself. His panentheism envisions a God distinct but connected to us and human beings that reflect this God in their interconnectedness. Pullman even drags in central but often neglected doctrines of Christianity, like the goodness of the body, the belief in the unity of the body and soul, and the Trinity, in order to express this vision. Pullman-the-atheist, who wants "to undermine the basis of Christian belief," must surely be a bit embarrassed by Pullman-the-writer, who uses such classical and orthodox Christian beliefs to tell his story, coupling them with the edgier, more contemporary work of liberation and feminist theologians. What Pullman has accomplished through this epic story is a task that has largely eluded scholars who adopt a panentheistic vision, at least beyond the ivory tower. Pullman has vividly introduced his millions of readers to the beguiling notion of *a people made of God.*[9]

What is your opinion? A man had two sons. He came to the first and said, "Son, go out and work in the vineyard today." He said in reply, "I will not," but afterwards he changed his mind and went. The man came to the other son and gave the same order. He said in reply, "Yes, sir," but did not go. Which of the two did his father's will?"

They answered, "The first."

JESUS TO HIS DISCIPLES (MATTHEW 21:28–31)

PART TWO

Divine Ambiguities

When Mary Malone is telling Will and Lyra the story of how she lost her faith, she explains that she left her religious order but continued as a scientist so she "wouldn't have to think about good and evil" (AS, 446). After studying dark matter, she discovered that it was conscious, and when she is then told by this dark matter to aid Will and Lyra, destroy her research before others find it, and leave her world to travel to the world of the kindly wheeled creatures called the *mulefa*, she feels she must reflect on right and wrong, good and bad. In a seemingly simple exchange, Mary says to Will, "And I came to believe that good and evil are names for what people do, not for what they are. All we can say is that this is a good deed, because it helps someone, or that's an evil one, because it hurts them" (AS, 447). This statement captures a profound and yet familiar understanding of good and evil woven throughout Pullman's trilogy: evil destroys us; good fulfills us.[1]

Yet Pullman does not leave us with a slogan of good and evil, assuming we can easily understand and apply it. He is not naïve. In *His Dark Materials,* the good and evil often look peculiar. He makes rebellious angels into heroes, and he makes his God a villain. The heroine—Lyra—is a liar. Her friend Will is a murderer. The Church is terribly corrupt, and witches and ex-nuns have an essential role in the salvation of the universe. Even science is not exempt, and although it is a force for good in Will's world, as it empowers Mary to understand and communicate with dark matter, its practitioners in Lyra's world devise bombs and experiment on children. Pullman forces his readers to look under superficial notions of good and evil at every turn.

And what do we discover beyond these superficial appearances? Freedom. The Authority and his Regent try to deprive every other creature of it. Scientists try to cut it out. People manipulate others into giving it up. Lyra and Will not only fight for freedom but need it to become victorious. Mary Malone, Iorek the armored bear, the Texan Lee Scoresby, Will's father the explorer John Parry, the witch Serafina Pekkala, and the courageous Gallivespians, Tailys and Salmakia, all freely choose to help preserve freedom for all by protecting Lyra and Will.

Ultimately, freedom is not an end for selfish purposes; it is *for* the service of others. All of Lyra's friends use freedom, not to secure their own interests—even Iorek, who insists that bears only side with what gives "advantage to the bears" (AS, 112)—but for the good of Lyra and Will and, through them, the good of all. Freedom, as necessary and inviolable as it is, is to be used to love others. Freedom is not just a freedom from restrictions and an invitation to do whatever one wants but rather a force that comes with responsibility to choose what benefits the lives of others.

Pullman's ideas about good, evil, freedom, and love are found in the bones, blood, and sinew of his characters and so are not abstractions but lived realities in the context of his story.[2] What follows in the next three chapters is our exploration of Pullman's ethics, and, as with Pullman's understanding of God, how his ethics give way to a very Christian understanding of good and evil.

Here in the city that was both hers and not hers,
danger could look friendly, and treachery smiled
and smelled sweet.

LYRA'S THOUGHTS ON WILL'S WORLD (SK, 160)

CHAPTER

4

THE BEAUTY OF EVIL

Near the beginning of *The Golden Compass,* a female servant of Jordan College extracts Lyra from the rooftops, scrubs her knees and nails clean, and attempts to give her a veneer of civility by plunking her into a freshly pressed dress and blouse. After all signs of Lyra's hedonistic play are removed, she is escorted into a dining room full of neat, mannered, and terribly dull scholars. Only one person stands out: the stunning and young Mrs. Coulter. Her charm, elegance, and golden-haired monkey dæmon set her apart, especially from the other women, whose paltry dæmons reflect their frumpy attire.

THE DEVIL AND HER GOLDEN MONKEY

Lyra is captivated by Mrs. Coulter and agrees to leave Jordan College to become her assistant. Lyra learns about politics, navigation, and the North from this alluring, mysterious woman, but most of all she learns how to dress, bathe, talk, and act polite and gracious. Lyra's domestication lasts about a month and a half before her wild side—the part that compelled her to investigate the roofs and basement of Jordan College, fight with brickburners' children, and steal a Gyptian boat—rebels.

The conflict between Lyra and Mrs. Coulter comes to a head immediately before a party. Lyra wants to carry a purse. Mrs. Coulter says no. But what seems like a commonplace battle of wills between a child and an adult quickly turns into something terrifying and foreboding. In response to Lyra's intransigence, Mrs. Coulter's plush golden monkey leaps on Pantalaimon, pins him down, and slowly and methodically starts tearing off his ear, causing Lyra and her dæmon to cry out in fear. Defeated by this attack, Lyra agrees to put the purse away, and the monkey releases Pan and acts as if nothing happened. After the incident, Mrs. Coulter demands a kiss from Lyra as a sign of reconciliation, but what she really wants is to solidify Lyra's subservience. When Lyra leans in for the kiss, she notices for the first time that underneath Mrs. Coulter's perfume and powder is a faint, nonhuman, metallic smell.

The Latin root of the word *enchanting* means "to sing against," making enchanting an apt description of Mrs. Coulter. She is enchanting because her physique, talk, appearance, knowledge, and grace all "sing against" the fact that she is manipulating, self-serving, and cruel. Not surprisingly, her dæmon expresses these same qualities. His long and lush golden fur is so alluring that children cannot help but want to stroke it, despite the strong taboo in Lyra's Oxford against touching another's dæmon. Yet, like the woman whose soul he embodies, the animal underneath this exotic beauty is vicious. Together Mrs. Coulter and her monkey manipulate people with the beautiful lyricism of their mere presence, which comforts and soothes children like music. Even when Mrs. Coulter does good, which is not until the last book of *His Dark Materials* when she, together with Lord Asriel, sacrifice themselves to "save Lyra" (which many readers, including ourselves, debate in terms of its sincerity), her good action is still double-dealing: she lures Metatron—the Authority's Regent—into an apparent trap and then doubles back to betray him. For Mrs. Coulter, being good is only accomplished through betrayals layered upon other betrayals. At least in *His Dark Materials,* it seems that evil is Dark and cannot help but look lovely.

Mrs. Coulter's enchanting appearance and personality, paired with her cruelty and manipulation, is an example of Pullman's exploration of evil and deception. This depiction is not the only one or even the most clear-cut one. By *The Amber Spyglass,* Mrs. Coulter seems to have reformed her ways at least somewhat, as we encounter her caring and helping Lyra instead of wanting to kill Lyra to further her own career in the Church. Yet she does so by drugging her daughter and keeping her in a perpetually sedated state.

Pullman's most challenging example of evil is the Authority—God—and all of the Authority's minions and institutions. It is the most challenging because our default way of thinking about God is as a benevolent being. Yet, even as Pullman's story mounts evil upon evil on the camp who sides with the Authority, his criticisms seems to echo the very same criticisms found in the prophetic tradition of Christianity.

So Many Wolves in Sheep's Clothing

In his writings about religion, Karl Marx showed how what religions purport to be good and true is often used by people to justify or protect their own self-interest. Marx said religion was the "opium of the people" because he saw how many rich and powerful people used it to keep themselves rich and powerful. "You might be suffering and poor now," the wealthy would say to their servants and slaves, "but you will get your reward in the afterlife." Although this statement is true in the sense that Christians believe in a Heaven where God blesses the poor and ends the suffering of all, the danger is that when the belief in an afterlife convinces the oppressed to endure unjust conditions, it becomes a false belief. In Marx's case, the afterlife is no longer about Heaven and God's love but a myth that serves to keep people in their place. In short, for Marx, how a concept is put into practice—for example, if it can be employed to foster oppression—tells us more about its truthfulness than the idea on its own.[1]

We all have seen examples of just this sort of hypocrisy, particularly in the realm of religion. Jesus had little patience for it, especially in religious leaders. They "preach but they do not practice," he said. "They tie up heavy burdens (hard to carry) and lay them on people's shoulders, but they will not lift a finger to move them. All their works are performed to be seen" (Matthew 23:2–7). Jesus excoriates such people for using religion to glorify themselves rather than to help others, for caring more about their own wealth and power than about justice and peace. Some religious leaders of Jesus' time were doing just what Marx warned about: using ostensibly truthful words as masks to divert attention from and justify the evil that they do.

Pullman's Authority is a classic example of someone spouting truths for the baser purposes of building power. The Authority portrays himself as good: the compassionate god that created the universe and all creatures in it, who watches over people, and protects and disciplines them so that they too can become good. But the Authority is only pretending to be the all-powerful and all-knowing creator. In actuality, he shares much in common with Mrs. Coulter, who pretends to care for the children she lures into captivity only to hand them over to the General Oblation Board for vicious experiments. Pullman infuses the Authority, not with knowledge, goodness, and love but with a despicable nature: an unyielding desire to oppress, rule, and control every conscious being in every universe. The Authority is even willing to torture and kill to expand and maintain his power.

Here, Pullman is playing with some classical themes about evil. Evil often masquerades as good, appearing beautiful, appealing, or strong. Barefaced evil cannot readily be done. Most often, if people *want* to do something wicked, they often must try to justify their actions by cloaking them in goodness. These ideas are embodied in such diverse stories as the sirens in the *Odyssey*, the step mother in *Snow White*, Mr. Wickham in *Pride and Prejudice*, and even Shift the ape and Puzzle the donkey in C. S. Lewis's *The Last Battle*. This notion of evil is vocalized by the ancient Jewish prophets and eventually appropriated by Christians. But before we explore Christianity's take on evil, Pullman still has more to say.

Does Believing It Is Good Make It So?

This first kind of deceit—evil masquerading as good—leads to a second kind for Pullman: people who accept the lies and do evil while believing their actions to be good. This type of evil occurs in *The Golden Compass* when the Church undertakes experiments designed to eradicate sin, yet requires in turn the destruction of Dust and the violent and sometimes lethal separation of children from their dæmons. It is through this particular combination of deceits at Bolvangar—not only evil masquerading as good but also evil that is *believed* to be good—that Pullman explores the sometimes imperceptible line between good and evil.

Throughout the trilogy, people who have devoted themselves to the Authority have accepted his lies as truths and live according to them. No group follows the Authority more blindly than those working at Bolvangar—the scientific station in the North run by an arm of the Church called the General Oblation Board. Also known as the Gobblers (from the committee's name—Gobblers—and from the fact that they "gobble up" children), members of the General Oblation Board refer to Bolvangar simply as "the Station," a name that whitewashes any trace of malice or wrongdoing. Yet Bolvangar, the name given to the Station by those who live nearby is more appropriate, as *Bolvangar* means "field of evil."

When Mrs. Coulter first appears at Bolvangar, we learn that she is not only the head of the General Oblation Board, but she is overseeing the brutal experiments on children conducted there. She uses her charm and, occasionally, the indulgence of chocolate, to attract prepubescent children—children whose dæmons have not yet settled. These youngsters are gathered mostly from the fringes of society. They are Gyptian children, homeless children, children of neglectful parents, poor children—children, in short, whose absences will either likely be welcomed or unnoticed by their families, and will probably go unreported in any case. And Mrs. Coulter has them shipped in bulk from England to Bolvangar. Because they live on the margins of society and come from poor, powerless families, liberation theologian Dorothee Söelle would call these children "replaceables." For her, replaceability is the first quality of oppression, so replaceables are individuals who, tragically, are treated not as unique but as expendable.[2]

The scientists that run the Station initially treat the children relatively well, giving them things they lacked in their earlier lives: food, shelter, toys to play with, and activities to perform. At first glance, the only price these children pay for such creature comforts is submitting to medical examinations, which seem to involve little more than weighing and measuring the child and his or her dæmon. Yet, eventually, this treatment gives way to intercision—the severing of the intimate bond connecting child and dæmon—and, in the case of little Tony Makarios, ultimately death.

This violent operation is the brainchild of Mrs. Coulter, and her motivations are clear. The Church has determined that Dust is far from divine. Rather, it is the physical manifestation of original sin. As such, it is evidence of human corruption, as Dust settles on humans primarily after puberty, with the onset of sexual maturation. The Bolvangar experiments of Mrs. Coulter and the General Oblation Board are designed to keep Dust from settling on people. If that can be accomplished, the effects of original sin can be staunched.

Children are the most obvious candidates for intercision, because once people have reached puberty, it is too late to stop Dust and sin from settling on them. At Bolvangar, scientists discover that if they separate a child and its dæmon before the dæmon settles on a particular form, Dust does not settle on the person at all. Mrs. Coulter and the scientists alike assume that they are doing a great good by stopping evil and corruption in the world. They are doing what the Authority wants them to do: ending sin.

Intercision is perhaps the most profound evil found in all of *His Dark Materials* and clearly is the most reprehensible dimension of the first book of the trilogy—*The Golden Compass*. The people and dæmons who have been severed and live beyond intercision are pitiful creatures. As Lyra journeys northward with the Gyptians, the alethiometer tells her to rescue a boy—the same Tony Makarios mentioned earlier—who is trapped in a fish house at a village far off the route she is traveling. Lyra gets Lord Faa's permission to ride the armored bear Iorek Byrnison to this village and back in search of him.

When Lyra arrives, she finds the villagers terrified of the fish house and hostile to the boy inside it. Lyra is initially perplexed by this cruelty, but when she finds Tony, she understands their fear. Lyra discovers Tony clutching a dead fish as if it were his dæmon and asking "Where's Ratter?" In other words, Tony is perpetually searching for his precious dæmon, which the scientists at Bolvangar have cut away. He is directionless, confused, and incapable of acting independently. He has lost his sense of self and will die soon after Lyra finds him. With his dæmon cut away, he has been made less than human. In fact, Pullman refers to him as a half-boy. But all this was done in the name of the Good, in an effort to reverse the effects of original sin.

In order to make sense of just how cruel is the separation of human beings from their daemons in the universe of *His Dark Materials*, we must consider how Pullman endows human beings with the threefold nature we discussed in Chapter Three. In the trilogy, every person has a body, a soul, and a spirit, which together generate and sustain conscious-ness, creativity, and freedom—everything we associate with human life. These activities—thinking, acting, and reflecting—are precisely what generates and are supported by Dust. Inter-cision is evil because it turns human beings into shadows of themselves, transforming boys into half-boys and girls into half-girls, and severs them from their union with the divine, with Dust.

The ability of a person's beliefs to justify evil—in this case, beliefs in original sin and the value of intercision—is one of the reasons that liberation theologians beginning with Gus-tavo Gutierrez in the early 1970s followed in the wake of Karl Marx: they emphasized the consequences of ideas, not sim-ply the ideas only in theory.[3] Truth is measured by how ideas affect us in everyday experience—in the here and now and under *these* particular conditions of suffering and oppression. Jesus' continual refrain in the gospels is to measure people by their "fruits": do they feed the hungry, give drink to the thirsty, shelter the homeless, visit the sick and imprisoned, preach the good news to the poor? If people act in this way, their words about God are trustworthy, and their interpreta-tions of the Word of God—the Bible—are trustworthy as well.

Feminist theologian Letty M. Russell recognizes that many of the ways the scriptures and traditions of Christianity have been interpreted and applied across history are highly problematic for those who are working to combat racism, sexism, and poverty, among other injustices. "The symbols and words of church *traditions* have become so encrusted by their formation in a sexist and racist Western culture that the language sometimes becomes a barrier to communication," she writes. "For those who experience the barriers of exclusion on the basis of racial or biological origin, the past becomes useless when language, as well as history and myth, is used to reinforce these patterns of prejudice."[4]

Within liberation theology, neither tradition nor scripture is ever simply *received* without question. It is assessed by its fruits: Is it oppressive or does it empower? Does it look good on paper only or in practice, too?

SATAN'S PROPHET

Pullman's theme that evil often masquerades as good is, of course, a classical Christian theme. It is also found in the work that inspired Pullman's *His Dark Materials*: Milton's *Paradise Lost*. In *Paradise Lost*, Satan's original name is Lucifer, which means "light-bearer." Lucifer is the first, most glorious, most powerful, and most intelligent of all of the angels. When God tells Lucifer that angels are to serve human beings, Lucifer rebels, saying, "I will not serve," and once the greatest of all angels, he now becomes the worst, and recruits other angels to follow him and to wage war on heaven. Pullman, of course, reinterprets Lucifer's rebellion so that Lucifer is on the side of humanity, and God is on the side of evil. (We agree, though, that Pullman frequently and publicly contends that William Blake's belief that Milton was secretly "of the

Devil's party"—because Milton portrays Lucifer so convincingly—was spot on.)

Like Milton, Pullman believes that evil is often disguised as good and, in fact, *requires* such deception. Evil is the suppression of freedom, the deprivation of the body, the failure to be kind. It is any action that partially or completely kills others. No person would willingly submit to manipulation, slavery, or murder, so people dress evil up to look enchanting and smell sweet. In Pullman's world, evil offers you chocolate, or says it is a benevolent deity, or insists it is just a small cut that will not hurt. Only in the guise of good are evil beings able to impose their will upon others and dupe people into believing that the evil they do is really good.[5]

While Pullman claims he is on the side of Satan, in *His Dark Materials*, "Satan" does not advocate evil. The Authority's adversaries (for the word *Satan* actually means adversary)—are fighting for freedom, creativity, human flourishing, and love. "Satan" actually seems to be on the side we normally think of as God's; in championing the views of this Satan, Pullman seems to be playing the role of Satan's prophet.

The default way of thinking about a prophet is "one who predicts the future." A prophet prophesies and sees into the future and warns us what is coming. The biblical notion of the prophet is much different. The word *prophet* comes from the Greek word that means "to speak out." This understanding is a more accurate understanding of the role of a prophet. A prophet speaks out against the wrongs of a society, how the just are marginalized and the weak oppressed, how religious and political leaders do what is evil and pretend to be good. A prophet will tell people what is right and wrong, even if doing so leads to his or her own imprisonment or death. In short, a prophet's primary role is not to be a seer of future calamities but an oracle about current wrongs and woes.[6]

The prophet Isaiah is a good example here. The first third of Isaiah's writings address the southern half of the kingdom of Israel before it is conquered in 587 B.C. Isaiah warns the leaders that it is their moral corruption that will lead to their downfall: "Woe to those who enact unjust statutes and who write oppressive decrees, depriving the needy of judgment and robbing my people's poor of their rights, making widows their plunder, and orphans their prey!" (Isaiah 10:1–2). Isaiah warns that these politicians and priests do not stop with these evils but also, "call evil good and good evil . . . change darkness into light and light into darkness . . . [and] . . . change bitter into sweet, and sweet into bitter" (Isaiah 5:19). Finally, these people do those despite their belief in God: "this people draws near with words only and honors me with their lips alone, though their hearts are far from me . . ." (Isaiah 29:13).

Isaiah goes after the people for not only doing wrong but also trying to portray it as right and using religion to do so. Although his criticism was directed toward an event of ancient history, Isaiah's words could be words in *His Dark Material*. His warnings about those who deprive the needy, rob the poor, and prey on orphans could be those of the Gyptians, whose children were among the replaceables exploited by the Church. Or Isaiah's criticism of those who call evil good and good evil is almost exactly Lyra's realization at the end of *The Golden Compass*: "Because if [the Oblation Board, the Church, Mrs. Coulter, and Lord Asriel] all think Dust is bad, it must be good."

These similarities in Isaiah's speeches about evil and Pullman's depiction of evil make the difference seem hardly a difference at all. Like all the great prophets, Isaiah insisted that he was speaking not his words but God's. He prefaced almost all his criticisms with the phrase, "thus says the Lord." Isaiah points to the evils in the world and names them as evil because they oppose God and God's design. Pullman's characters stand in opposition to God as the Authority, so they would not use Isaiah's words. Yet people like Lyra, Will, Lee Scoresby, the Witches, the Gallivespians, and John Parry do point to and name evil precisely because it is in opposition to freedom, kindness, and creativity, and most of all because it opposes Dust. Were Pullman to write like a prophet, the logical replacement of Isaiah's phrase might seem to be, "thus says Dust." This phrasing, though, seems to set Dust apart from and above human beings, practically turning it into another Authority seeking our obedience. Instead, the better replacement would be, "thus says Satan." Satan means adversary, so Pullman would not be setting up a single, rival god but rather pointing to and advocating for any and all adversaries of tyranny, cruelty, and deception.

Pullman, in adopting a prophetic mode of criticism in his books, seems not only to situate himself squarely in the Christian tradition but within Christian liberation theology. Liberation theology often turns to the prophets as model believers because the prophets call attention to what is wrong here and now and demand that it be fixed.[7] The prophets challenge people and societies to change. They advocate for the "widows and orphans"—the replaceables of their day and age. The prophets even go after people who profess faith in God "with their lips alone" and fail to put their faith into practice. Pullman's depiction of evil, as well as his opposition to it, sets up his story as a kind of classical prophetic criticism of religion, a kind with which liberation theologians could readily agree.

To live is to change, and to be perfect
is to have changed often.

JOHN HENRY NEWMAN, NINETEENTH-CENTURY ANGLICAN

CONVERT TO CATHOLICISM[1]

THE GOOD THAT
MAKES US HUMAN

Iorek Byrnison, Lyra's beloved *panserbjørne,* or armored bear, introduced to us in *The Golden Compass,* is the most significant intelligent animal hero in the trilogy and one of the most morally ambiguous. His massive figure resembles a polar bear: his fur is white, and his black eyes and nose adorn an expressionless face. Like other bears, he hunts for seal and fish, yet Iorek is more than his animal nature. He uses his opposable thumbs to score, bend, and reshape metal into armor, adding significant protection to an already formidable arsenal of teeth, claws, raw strength, and shrewd intelligence. The panserbjørne primarily live alone, but they do have a political structure, a kingdom called Svalbard, with a king—Iofur Raknison, for a time—and an ethic governing their conduct that includes a ban on killing their own kind (in almost every situation). Once hired, armored bears do not go back on their word but fulfill their obligations to the letter. Only death keeps them from doing their jobs.

Know Thyself, Be Thyself

One day, not far into Lyra's journey North, she and Farder Coram, the wise Gyptian who helps her learn to read the alethiometer, first encounter Iorek. At the time, Iorek is an indentured servant and, despite his massive size and ferocious maw, he spends his days doing trivial metalworking for the sledge depot in Trollesund—the main port of Lapland and the location of the witch Consulate. Iorek is paid for his work in food and spirits, eating only to keep his strength up for work during the day and drinking himself into a stupor at night. Seeing such a majestic creature in such a pitiful state stirs deep empathy in Lyra, and Farder Coram almost insults Iorek when he asks why a panserbjørne would be reduced to such unimportant work.

How and why has Iorek, a former panserbjørne king, lost his dignity?

Iorek is living in Trollesund—an outpost near Bolvangar— because he has been exiled from his home, Svalbard, for fighting and killing another bear. The panserbjørne have rules and rituals governing combat among bears. Death, if it comes during the fight, occurs by accident. Once the winner is clear, the defeated bear is supposed to give signals conceding defeat, and the superior bear, in turn, is supposed to stop his aggression. In Iorek's case, Iorek *had* demonstrated his superiority in combat over a fellow bear. Given the rules of combat, that bear *should* have signaled his submission, but he did not. So Iorek continued to demonstrate his superiority; the other bear continued to refuse to submit, and the fight escalated until Iorek killed him.

Even though the challenging bear refused to respect the panserbjørne rules for combat, Iorek should have relented. When he did not, he was banished from Svalbard and stripped of all rights to live with his kind, including his position as their king. Worst of all, upon arriving in Trollesund, Iorek is tricked into losing his armor, which, as he explains to Lyra "is his soul, just as your dæmon is your soul" (GC, 196–197)—the panserbjørne equivalent of a soul or, in Lyra's world, a dæmon. So the townspeople are able to pacify and enslave him. Without his armor, he cannot fight, and if he cannot fight he is not truly a panserbjørne. In Iorek's mind, if he cannot count himself a panserbjørne, then he is nothing. No wonder Lyra and Farder Coram find Iorek in such a miserable state when they first meet him.

When Lyra expresses concern about the fact that the people of Trollesund tricked him into losing what amounts to his soul, Iorek insists that armored bears cannot be deceived. "We see tricks and deceit as plain as arms and legs," he explains (GC, 226). Yet how else could Iorek have lost his armor? Strangely enough, Lyra herself commits an even more profound act of deceit at the hands of an armored bear. After she is captured and taken to Svalbard at the end of *The Golden Compass,* she confronts the bears' new king, Iofur Raknison. Iofur is a peculiar monarch who erects an ice castle, talks of opening a university, replaces the traditional sky iron armor of the panserbjørne with armor of more ornamental metals, and, strangest of all, carries around a stuffed doll resembling Mrs. Coulter. In an effort to feign humanness, he pretends the doll is his dæmon. Iofur's obsession with making the bears more human by replacing the bears' ways with human ways is Iofur's Achilles heel. Aware of this weakness, Lyra tricks Iofur into agreeing to fight Iorek. The trick begins with a lie. Lyra lies to Iofur, telling him that if he kills Iorek she will become his dæmon. Because Iofur so desperately wants a dæmon, he falls for this trick, agreeing to let Iorek back into Svalbard for the sole purpose of fighting him to the death.

During Iofur's battle with Iorek, Iofur makes a second and more costly mistake. At a critical moment, Iorek appears to be hurt on his left side. Noticing this apparent injury, Iofur showers Iorek with taunts and blows. But Iorek's retreat is nothing more than an attempt to find solid ground from which he can lunge at Iofur with his perfectly strong and healthy left arm. When Iorek does attack, he rips away Iofur's bottom jaw, leaving his tongue hanging out and dangling from his mouth. Iofur is dead seconds after he realizes this deception.

Here again, a panserbjørne is deceived. But how can these bears be deceived when, supposedly, it is impossible to deceive them? Serafina Pekkala, Lyra's closest witch friend, grasps the logic behind this apparent loophole succinctly. "When bears act like people perhaps they can be tricked," she says. "When bears act like bears, perhaps they can't" (GC, 317). Iorek could only be deceived when he was drunk—when he was acting like a human and not an armored bear. Once he stopped pretending to be human, his resistance to deception was restored, as was his dignity and his rightful place as king of the bears. Iofur could only be deceived because he wanted more than anything else to be human. But this desire put the whole kingdom of the bears in jeopardy. Only when Iorek retook the throne were the panserbjørnes able to restore their dignity and be who they truly were meant to be.

The Good Is That Which Uniquely Perfects Us

What we learn from the predicaments of Iorek and Iofur—that dignity comes from being true to who you are—reveals yet another insight about distinguishing the good from the bad in the universe of *His Dark Materials*. What we are—be that human, panserbjørne, Gallivespian, angel, or witch—determines what is good for us. Each creature, each species, each community—all created things—are *intended* to live a certain kind of life in the universe. When we fulfill the purpose for which we are created, we are doing what is right. Thomas Aquinas, the medieval Christian theologian, gave his general definition of *the good* as "that which perfects or fulfills" something. He said that if we look at the nature or essence of a thing, then it is possible to figure out what will lead to genuine flourishing for this object, what will perfect it, what will fulfill it, and what is *good* for it.[2]

If goodness depends on a being's nature, then because beings are so different, what is good will have to be different for each. Bear armor might perfect a panserbjørne but not a human or a witch or a worm. A dæmon may be able to travel hundreds of miles away from a witch, but this same act will be excruciating, perhaps even deadly, for a human in Lyra's world. Even when we are acting from within our natures—as humans or bears or even angels—discerning what is good for us is not always so obvious. In certain situations a lie might be the best decision and in others killing, but by changing the circumstances, acts that were in one moment permissible or even laudable may in another moment suddenly become reprehensible and unforgivable. So not only do differences among creatures affect the nature of the good, but the different situations in which even creatures of the same species may find themselves can affect the nature of the good.

These qualifications cannot be neglected, but they do not imply that the good is arbitrary or a personal preference. Beings are of a particular kind and so have a particular nature. People find themselves in concrete circumstances and, in those circumstances, the good is discernable. Pullman is very sensitive to those oppressed throughout the universe—children, Gallivespians, Gypsies—and is aware of how circumstance shapes what we should and should not do, but Pullman still believes there are actions that are good and right and true and actions that are not. While any number of characters exemplify this idea, Lord Asriel provides a particularly complex and rich illustration.

Lord Asriel: The Embodiment of Human Perfection

Like Iorek, Lord Asriel is not an easy character to understand. Is he a villain as terrible as the Authority or a daring hero bent on saving the universe? At the beginning of *The Golden Compass,* he seems arrogant and cold. He thanks Lyra for her warning about the poison in his Tokay by roughly grabbing her arm and chastising her for being in the room. He then proceeds to use Lyra as a spy, imprisoning her in a wardrobe and *rewarding* her by reducing her punishment for sneaking into the room. All and all, he acts the fun-loving uncle you cannot wait to have visit.

Lord Asriel does not become a more likeable figure as *The Golden Compass* continues, however. He bullies the scholars at

Jordan College into giving him funds for his work. He turns out to be Lyra's father but has little interest in taking responsibility for his child. Even when Lyra confronts him about being her father, he seems nonplussed, saying, "Yes, so what?" His most horrendous act is the killing of Roger. At the moment a person and dæmon are separated through intercision, a large amount of energy is released. The scientists of Bolvangar were uninterested in this fact, focusing instead on stopping Dust from settling on children. Asriel, however, created a device that would harness this energy and generate an explosion strong enough to rip a hole in the fabric of the universe, opening up pathways between the parallel worlds. It is no wonder that Asriel's name is "an alternative spelling of Azrael, the angel in Jewish and Muslim mythology who severs the soul from the body; that is, the angel of death."[3]

After Lyra rescued the children from Bolvangar and helped restore Iorek to his throne, she took Roger and set off to free Lord Asriel, whom she thought imprisoned on Svalbard. While technically he was being held by the panserbjørne, he was living in a palace; he had the freedom to do what he wanted and get what he wanted. He had even chosen the location of his "prison" to help him run the experiments needed to effectively use his explosive device.

When Lyra shows up with Roger, Lord Asriel seems shocked, stumbling over, crying out "no, no, no" in despair. We discover later that Lord Asriel believed he was going to have to use Lyra to detonate his device, but when he sees Roger clutching Lyra, almost hidden, he regains his composure, realizing that he can "use" the other child. When Lyra is still asleep, Asriel takes Roger to a place where the boundaries between the worlds are the thinnest. Lyra tries to rescue

Roger, but is too late. In a startlingly cruel moment in the trilogy, Asriel severs Roger and his dæmon, killing them to set off the explosion and open a bridge to other worlds. He then crosses, leaving his stunned and horrified daughter watching from afar and abandoning his former lover Mrs. Coulter, even as she begs him to remain with her.

A bully, an absent father, a murderer for his own ends, Lord Asriel has to be evil, does he not? In *The Subtle Knife*, we know from Thorold, Asriel's manservant, what Asriel is up to: "He's gone a-searching for the dwelling place of the Authority Himself, and he's a-going to destroy him" (SK, 45–46). Asriel's cold, callous acts are apparently for a good purpose—to defeat the tyranny of the Authority, to return freedom, peace, and creativity to people, to enable Dust to once again thrive. His end is good, but his means are questionable, so should Asriel simply learn that the ends do not justify the means? Perhaps. But he does live in a strange time: people are assaulted on all sides by the Church, live in a world lorded over by a jealous Authority, and are coming under greater control by the Authority's regent, Metatron. What can one do in such a circumstance?

Dietrich Bonhoeffer was a Lutheran minister in Nazi Germany. All churches during that time were required to swear loyalty to the führer and the Nazi party. When he and many of his colleagues refused to do so, they had to go underground, becoming the Confessing Church. All around, Bonhoeffer saw the evils of the Nazi party and Adolf Hitler usurping people's freedom and persecuting the Jews. He had resisted being co-opted by the party but did not feel it was enough. He had to do something. He became involved with a plot to assassinate Hitler. He knew, as a Christian, that killing was wrong, but he also knew, as a Christian, that allowing this evil to continue was wrong. He chose to act anyway, though the plot was not ultimately successful. Hitler continued his rise to power, the Holocaust continued, and Bonhoeffer was imprisoned and, eventually, hanged.[4]

Nowhere in *His Dark Materials* does Asriel seem to ruminate over his decision to kill Roger; he expressed no concern or regret about the loss of life, so, in that sense, his act differs from Bonhoeffer's. Still, the circumstances are similar—the tyranny, the control, the decreasing number of viable alternatives. Killing is obviously wrong, but how else does one open up the worlds in order to fight with the Authority. So Asriel is good, right?

To take on the Authority and Metatron, the Authority's regent, Asriel amasses an enormous army, drawing on creatures from across the universes, creatures marginalized and persecuted by the Church. He builds forges, the likes of which no world had seen. He develops an intention craft—a helicopter-like device that runs on the power flowing between human and dæmon and is controlled through intentions. His fortress sits on the crest of mountain with a cavern below for all the metallurgy. Asriel builds an army to do what he desires, just as the Authority has built an army over the course of time to impose his will. Is there a difference between these acts? Asriel, of course, claims to be against the domination and control of the Authority. He even seems to embody this in his leadership when he consults and collaborates with his generals instead of dictating orders to them. He wants to set up a Republic of Heaven—an alternative to the Authority's Kingdom of Heaven and a place of freedom and knowledge built in a single world, where people from all worlds can come together. Is this not different from the Authority?

Before the ghost of Will's father, John Parry, leaves the Land of the Dead, he tells Lyra and Will that, "Lord Asriel's great enterprise will fail in the end . . . we have to build the Republic of Heaven where we are, because for us there is no elsewhere" (AS, 363). Even with the best of intentions, Asriel is trying to set up an institution spanning the universes, to bring the Republic from above down to the people. He will fight and win, and the people of all the universes will join his movement. In structure, even if not in theory, Asriel's Republic functions much like the Authority's Kingdom. It is imposed, however benevolently or malevolently, from above. In fighting the Authority, Asriel has adopted the tactics of the Authority he so despises, and so becomes more and more like the Authority. John Parry suggests this loophole and says that the true Republic cannot be imposed, because people must be free. The Republic must arise from all the people in their own worlds and in their own way working together. If Asriel truly wants to resist the Authority, he must not only conceive of the Republic differently from the Kingdom but build it differently, with freedom instead of force. So, again, Asriel seems bad, imposing his designs on the people like the Authority.

By the end of the story though, Asriel has changed one last time. He realizes that it is not his power that will defeat the Authority, but Lyra: "Our Republic might have come into being for the sole purpose of helping her . . ." (AS, 379). With this insight, Asriel also grasps what he must do: "But my part is nearly over. It's my daughter who has to live, and it's our task to keep all the forces of the Kingdom away from her" (AS, 379). Asriel must here use force but not to conquer. He can defeat the Authority only by protecting and safeguarding Lyra, helping her to be free so that the universe might be free. On behalf of this knowledge, Asriel leaves his military command center and heads out onto the battlefield where he encounters Metatron, who has been duped by Mrs. Coulter into believing she is betraying Asriel. Asriel fights with Metatron and wins, not by his brawn but by clinging to the angel and dragging him into a bottomless abyss. Asriel does kill, yet we feel that at last Asriel has figured out what it means to be good. He kills not to further his own ends (like with Roger) or to build his own Republic (as with the battle being waged against the Authority) but to protect others, especially Lyra, so that they might live in greater freedom.

With this scene, Asriel has moved from the distant and domineering uncle and scholar to a father who sacrifices his own life for the good of his daughter and the universe. He has made and remade himself thorough the story and revealed through the process what is good for human beings. Power to control and dominate brings cruelty to others and turns one into another Authority. Power used to protect and care for others may require self-sacrifice, and it is this willingness to give in the service of others that ultimately builds the Republic where human beings can flourish. Perhaps the most important revelation of human good in this instance is that we must strive with all our strength of mind and will to do what is right and realize that in doing so we will make many mistakes; it is precisely these mistakes that lead us to what is truly good. Asriel set off to bring an end to the Authority and used all his power to do so. He was by no means perfect, but the desiring and the mistakes led him to what ultimately needed to be done. He is ultimately able to do a truly good act, not because he is without fault but because he grows and learns from his faults, though indeed they are many and difficult to forgive, despite this final, heroic deed.

Pullman's Christian Good

Pullman's notion of the good is another example of the Christian worldview embedded throughout *His Dark Materials*. The good is not some inert object to be possessed by people, but, to borrow from Aquinas again, it is that which helps us flourish. In the examples of Iorek and Asriel, we find the command that we must figure out what we are, be true to this understanding, strive with all our might to do so, while resisting the temptation to fret about the inevitable mistakes and instead learn from them, grow, and be free.

Michael Himes, a Christian theologian and professor at Boston College, summarizes this understanding of the good when he writes that human beings are made such that they glorify God through the use of their freedom.[4] Animals and plants, he believes, give glory to God by just acting on their biological processes. Animals should live and procreate. Plants should grow and photosynthesize. Angels are beautiful creatures of impressive intellect and strong will. They are made to serve God in their splendor and majesty. Himes says that humans, though, are to serve God in the "tangle of our minds." Humans are given reason and freedom to creatively respond to God. People are not meant to be docile, flaccid creatures, but dynamic and imaginative. Himes's insistence on human freedom harkens back to Jesus' parable of the three servants. Each one got a few coins to look after. Two of them invested the coins in various enterprises and were rewarded for their efforts. The only one of the three that is punished is the one who did not do anything with the coins. The one who did not use his freedom to respond to the gift he was given. Even the notion of mistakes is captured in the Christian tradition. Himes notes that in Easter worship services, Christians often sing of the "happy fault," that is, the fall of Adam and Eve that brought God's Son to human beings. Himes, echoing this Christian understanding, notes that we should view all our sins in this manner—as happy faults that bring us to where we are today. The trick, Himes continues, is to keep on growing and learning from these mistakes, never becoming stagnant, always remaining restless.

Pullman's insistence that we must learn for ourselves who we are and that no one can force this upon us is a Christian theme picked up by many liberation theologians. People in power, whether the power is religious, political, or economic, tend to marginalize those without power. This process can lead the powerless to lose their sense of self-worth and importance and even their ability to resist the powerful. Liberation theologians believe that it is the experience of these people and their voice that should guide churches, governments, and business, but, to do so, these people need to reclaim their own sense of self. By insisting that the Republic of Heaven must be built by each one of us and cannot be constructed alone by even the most benevolent ruler, Pullman is insisting that each of us, even the mostly lowly and oppressed, is indispensable, or "irreplaceable," as Dorothee Söelle would insist. The powerless must reclaim responsibility for themselves and not hand it over to an Authority. The powerful, like Asriel, must learn to use their talents to protect others and to promote freedom, so that people do come to know themselves and be fully themselves.

Finally, Pullman's Asriel points to a greater truth about human goodness—one at the heart of the Christian faith. The end of Asriel's life suggests that the pinnacle of human flourishing is sacrificial love. Asriel hands over his life, not for his good but for the good of Lyra and the universe. With Asriel though, this theme is nascent. The tasks of Lyra and Will point to it more explicitly and are the subject of the next chapter.

But we en't old enough yet. We're only young . . .
We're too young . . . If poor Mr. Scoresby's
dead and Iorek's old . . . It's all coming
onto us, what's got to be done.

LYRA TO WILL BEFORE THEY SET OFF FOR
THE LAND OF THE DEAD (AS, 197)

6

LOVE FREES US

In *The Subtle Knife,* Will and Lyra stumble upon a throng of children in Cittàgazze dead set on the righteous execution of a cat—the same cat that walked from Will's Oxford into Cittàgazze, showing Will the first window between worlds. The Cittàgazze children believed the cat represented an evil almost on par with the specters and, without hesitation, were preparing to destroy it. After Will and Lyra stop them, the children realize that Will and Lyra are not from the city. When Will and Lyra get the subtle knife away from Tullio, the brother of Angelica and Pablo, thereby damning him to the zombie-like existence the specters inflict, the children, especially Tullio's siblings, threaten to kill Will and Lyra. The children would have succeeded if Serafina Pekkala had not intervened and rescued them. Based on this experience, Lyra concludes that, while she used to think that cruelty was foreign to children, "en't sure now. I never seen kids like that before, and that's a fact" (SK, 261).

Choosing Children

Pullman is no romantic when it comes to the innocence of children, and he's been quoted calling them "ignorant little savages" on more than one occasion.[1] His trilogy continually reminds the reader of their potential cruelty—a characteristic not unknown even to his heroine Lyra. In *The Golden Compass*, Lyra is described as a barbarian. "What she liked best was clambering over the College roofs with Roger, the kitchen boy who was her particular friend, to spit plum stones on the heads of passing Scholars or to hoot like owls outside a window where a tutorial was going on, or racing through the narrow streets, or stealing apples from the market, or waging war. Just as she was unaware of the hidden currents of politics running below the surface of College affairs, so the Scholars, for their part, would have been unable to see the rich seething stew of alliances and enmities and feuds and treaties that was a child's life in Oxford. Children playing together: how pleasant to see! What could be more innocent and charming?" (GC, 34–35).

Lyra may be charming, but she is not exactly innocent. She is a disruptive, warring, and thieving child, unusual only in the sense that she is a leader among children who willingly go along on her expeditions.

When Will witnesses the children attacking the cat, he is reminded of two things. First, children can be extremely brutal to anything and anyone different from themselves, as when Will's schoolmates discover his mother is not normal and decide to torment her as a result. Second, Will realizes something about himself far more chilling: that he is willing to hurt people.

"And he'd learned that the object of a school fight was not to gain points for style but to force your enemy to give in, which meant hurting him more than he was hurting you. He knew that you had to be willing to hurt someone else, too, and he'd found out that not many people were, when it came to it; but he knew that he was" (SK, 174). In Cittàgazze, Will again confronts the cruelty of children but also his own ability to hurt others when it is in his interest to do so (or, as in the case of the tortured cat, when it is in the interest of some higher good).

Plainly, Pullman does not believe children are innocents. They can be as cruel and violent as adults, if not more so. Yet it is not the might of Asriel and the Authority that will bring order to the world. It is not the power of witches or panser-bjørnes, nor the beauty of Mrs. Coulter, the wisdom of John Parry, or the cleverness of Lee Scoresby. In *His Dark Materials,* two children are destined to save the world, save Dust, and free the ghosts from the Land of the Dead, and it is neither their innocence nor the inherent goodness of children that makes them suitable for the task of salvation.

THE FAILURES OF POWER

As we discuss in Chapter Two, the central problem in Pullman's universe is a dictator-like Authority who masquerades as the all-powerful, all-knowing creator. Behind the Authority's lies is his desire to garner the slavish obedience of every being in creation, from angels to humans to Gallivespians. He does this in league with his Regent, the uber-angel Metatron, and by developing churches and magisteria to perpetuate his control in various worlds. This dictatorship is first and foremost at odds with human freedom. "Every little increase in human freedom," says Will's father John Parry, "has been fought over ferociously between those who want us to know more and be wiser and stronger, and those who want us to obey and be humble and submit" (SK, 320). The Authority obfuscates the truth and attempts to "suppress and control every natural impulse . . . [and] . . . obliterate every good feeling" (SK, 50). How can we conquer such totalitarianism?

Lord Asriel, Lyra's father, mounts one response. He journeys to another world in order to build a "colossal" fortress, surrounded by "the clang of hammers and the pounding of great mills" and forges, amassing an army of countless angels, machines, and creatures, all for the purpose of killing the Authority. Ruta Skadi, the witch queen who joins Asriel's side and was once his lover, believed that Asriel's forces could prevail because of his leadership and strong will. Yet although "Lord Asriel's army numbers millions . . . the forces of the Authority . . . number a hundred times as many" (SK, 273). Yet, in the end, the question of who has a bigger army does not get at the heart of the problem.

Neither Asriel's vast army nor his personal qualities are enough to defeat the Authority and bring about salvation of all the worlds and their creatures. For Pullman, it is not, as the historian Lord Acton would say, that "absolute power corrupts absolutely." True, Asriel and the Authority have immense power, but Will, who wields the æsahættr (the subtle knife, also called the God-destroyer, and arguably the most powerful weapon in the universe) is not corrupted. And Lyra converses with Dust, the source of all life, the real God, yet she is not corrupted either. For Pullman, power is neither corrupting nor liberating in and of itself.

The Virtue of Compassion

In *The Golden Compass,* Lyra is determined to find her dear friend Roger, who was carried off by the Gobblers, and as we already know, she heads North to find him. With the Gyptians and Iorek Byrnison, the armored bear, at her side, she attacks Bolvangar; tragically, she unwittingly leads Roger to his death at the hands of Lord Asriel. But it is her love of Roger and the sorrow over her betrayal of him that leads Lyra to a new world where she meets Mary Malone and Will. Will fights for the knife because he wants to help Lyra get her alethiometer. Lyra and Will are then driven to the Land of the Dead to help Roger, and, once there, they free all its ghosts. It is then through the love between Will and Lyra that the flow of Dust out of the world is stopped, and it is their compassionate decision never to see each other again that preserves Dust and brings peace to the dead.

Compassion, which literally means "to suffer with" and which the Greeks called *agapic* love, lies at the heart of the ethics of *His Dark Materials,* and the centrality of this virtue to Pullman's vision helps explain why children are harbingers of salvation. It is not that children are innocent and pure and thus better able to love. All human beings are capable of compassion. Unlike adults, however, children have access to little power and so are more likely to rely on love. Children can be cruel, to be sure. But if they want to be otherwise, and certainly if they want to save the world, they have little to work with other than self-giving, self-sacrificing *agapic* love.

Here again we see Pullman, rather than a Death-of-God novelist, instead relying on Christian themes to propel his trilogy—and his ethics—forward. It is a sad reflection on Christianity that its core teaching of love is not recognized by many non-Christians as its central characteristic. Early Christians were known for their care of the poor, the needy, widows, and orphans. It was their love that spoke to others. And at the Last Supper, Jesus encapsulated his teachings into this one word. "A new command I give you: Love one another. As I have loved you, so you must love one another" (John 13:34).

Pullman's emphasis on *agapic* love shares much, not only with Christianity in general but again with Christian liberation theology. Liberation theology says that this love is the key. Compassionate action is what should drive people to action, and this kind of action should, in turn, drive people's beliefs. Moreover, liberation theologians believe that the contemporary insights needed to discern what should be done and believed ought to be derived from those on the fringes of societies: the poor, the oppressed, the marginalized, minorities, women, and so on. These people have been deprived of power, education, and money, and because of this deprivation their discernment of the truth is less clouded and their willingness to act on the truth is less hindered. Children, of course, share much with these fringe populations; they are neither wealthy nor highly educated nor empowered. They are also more likely than the average adult to see and do what is right. In short, liberation theologians would see children as Pullman sees them: a population whose distance from power offers them a chance to love well. Here again, Pullman the atheist appears to be a pretty good Christian theologian.

WILL'S TASK

On Lyra's first excursion into Will's world, Sir Charles Latrom, known as Lord Boreal in Lyra's world, steals the alethiometer from her. He says he will give it back if she brings him a knife from the Torre degli Angeli in Cittàgazze. Will decides to help her, and as the two of them make their way up to the top of the tower they encounter Tullio, the older brother of Angelica and Paolo. Teetering on the edge of adulthood, Tullio has acquired the knife in order to defend himself from the specters that will come to attack him (as is their practice) as soon as he becomes an adult. As Will and Lyra free Giacomo Paradisi, whom Tullio has bound and injured, Tullio attacks them. Will repels the attack and seizes the knife, but not before he has lost two fingers on his left hand.

This seemingly accidental injury turns out to be the sign of the knife bearer. As Giacomo Paradisi, the previous knife bearer, explains to Will, "My time is over. . . . The knife knows when to leave one hand and settle in another. . . . I fought and lost the same fingers, [it is] the badge of the bearer" (SK, 180). Giacomo will soon die, but in the meantime, he quickly teaches Will about the knife: how it cuts through to other worlds and how it is Will's responsibility as its bearer to seal up the openings after he is done with them. Giacomo bemoans the facts that he has so little time to teach Will about the knife and that Will is so young. He concludes this short lesson by saying, "There is no time. You have come here for a purpose, and maybe you don't know what that purpose is, but the angels do who brought you here. Go. You are brave, and your friend is clever. And you have the knife. Go" (SK, 188).

Giacomo's assessment is accurate: with the knife, Will has acquired a purpose that is not yet clear to him. The assumption of most of the story's characters, from the angels Balthamos and Baruch to the Gallivespian spies, is that Will should go and fight on the side of Lord Asriel against the Authority because he holds the subtle knife—the æsahættr or

"God destroyer"—the only weapon that can enable Asriel to win his war against the Authority.

John Parry, Will's father, also holds this belief. Before Will was born, Parry left for an expedition in the North. Officially, he was performing scientific experiments, but unofficially he was searching for a window-like phenomenon. In the process, Parry unknowingly stumbled through a window into Lyra's world, never to return to his own. In Lyra's world, John became a famous scientist and learned much about the Authority, Lord Asriel's rebellion, and the subtle knife. He then set out to find the knife bearer and direct him to Lord Asriel.

Before Parry realizes that the knife bearer is his son, he tells Will to side with Lord Asriel. When he learns that Will has the knife, he insists that the knife "picked" Will and that it is Will's nature and destiny as "a warrior" to fight the battle against the Authority. Right after this speech, Parry is killed by the arrow of an avenging witch whose love John had rejected.

The weight of this destiny is no small thing. Everyone, including Will's father and the two greatest powers in the universe—Lord Asriel and the Authority—believe Will has been chosen to kill the Authority. Though this messianic burden may seem fated to many, it will not be taken up unless Will decides to do so. In the universe of *His Dark Materials,* Will is free to act as he sees fit. He is free to be selfish or to be compassionate.

LYRA'S TASK

Like Will, Lyra is equally free. After Lyra tells the ghosts that she and Will are going to try and lead them out of the Land of the Dead, a monk steps forward to denounce her. Lyra, he says, is an "evil girl," "an agent of the Evil One himself" who wants to "lead you to Hell!" (AS, 321). This monk has been so shaped by the falsehoods of the Authority and by a lifestyle—monasticism—that continually reinforces these falsehoods that he sees the pallid existence of the ghosts and the barrenness of their land as a "blessed place," even a "paradise, which to the fallen soul seems bleak and barren, but which the eyes of faith see as it is, overflowing with milk and honey and resounding with the sweet hymns of the angels" (AS, 320–321). This monk cannot see the cruelty of the harpies that rule over the Land of the Dead, the despondency of the ghosts, or the hollowness of the land. He cannot imagine anything better than what he sees around him. In Will and Lyra he sees only a threat, so he turns away from them "in horror and loathing" (AS, 321). The monk's environment has so shaped and determined him that he is not truly free to act, to think, or to see his circumstances as they are. Contrast the monk's environment with that of Lyra. Lyra grows up parentless at Jordan College. She is the responsibility of everyone, which means she is the responsibility of no one. She was supposed to be tutored by Jordan scholars, but often she frustrated their efforts. Given Lyra's desire to play and the scholars' interests in their own works, neither was eager to make the lessons happen and all were relieved when they stopped.

Even the witches' prophecy about Lyra, first revealed to the Gyptian Farder Coram by the Witches Consul, insists that she be innocent of real learning:

> The witches have talked about this child for
> centuries past . . . who has a great destiny that can
> only be fulfilled elsewhere—not in this world, but far

beyond. Without this child, we shall all die. So the witches say. But she must fulfill this destiny in ignorance of what she is doing, because only in her ignorance can we be saved. (GC, 176)

Lyra is the girl who is to save the world. Because she does not know of this prophesy, however, she will be left to respond as she sees fit to the situations in which she finds herself. The witches must keep quiet about her destiny; otherwise "it will all fail" (GC, 310). They can help Lyra but cannot interfere with her decisions. She can fulfill her destiny only by being free to make her own way.

Lyra's environment is a far cry from that of the monk. Where he is unable to think freely, Lyra is not just allowed but driven by her taste for adventure to be free. This degree of freedom does not come without danger. Lyra unwittingly chooses to betray Roger, for example. But her freedom to make mistakes also enables her to become aware of those around her who are suffering or in need. She hears Roger's pleas and sets out to find him. When she arrives in the Land of the Dead and sees the ghosts' misery, she does something to end it. She is free to think, feel, and act, and she uses this freedom to compassionate ends. But then again she has been raised in an environment conducive to freedom.

FATE

Liberation theology has long concerned itself with the ways that social structures affect and serve to oppress the most vulnerable. Why is it that a woman with the same job, work experience, and education as a male colleague will earn only seventy-three cents for every dollar that he earns? Why do African Americans make up 13 percent of the population but 60 percent of those on death row and 30 percent of those executed?[2] Why do children from upper-class families score better on standardized tests than those from working-class families? While choice and freedom play some role in these phenomena, the disparities cannot be attributed to individual effort alone. Social factors also generate these imbalances. Liberation theology sets as its aim, first, to uncover such structural inequalities (what it calls social sin) and, second, to change these social structures so as to undo their ill effects. The great Catholic social activist Dorothy Day captured liberation theologians' aim well, when she said that her Catholic Worker movement was trying to create a society where "it was easier to be good."[3]

When Pullman discusses various factors that restrict or enhance human freedom, he does not use terms like *social structures*. He focuses instead on the tension between destiny and freedom or nature and choice. The witches' prophecy surrounding Lyra seems to contradict itself. It describes Lyra's destiny yet calls for the witches to let her make her own decisions. As Lee Scoresby says to Serafina Pekkala after she explains the prophecy, "Are you telling me that she's just some kind of clockwork toy wound up and set going on a course she can't change?" (GC, 310). Serafina responds by saying, "We are all subject to the fates. But we must all act as if we are not." What Serafina refers to as "the fates" we have called environmental factors. Even though these factors (or fates) may restrict people in ways that compromise their ability to act, people are still responsible for acting toward the good. And even if it turns out that all our actions are determined by external influences, we must still act as if we have agency.

While Scoresby's discussion with Serafina turns on destiny and freedom, a similar conversation between John Parry and Will turns on nature and choice. Right before he is killed, Parry asks Will if he has fought and if he has won his fights. After Will answers yes to both, Parry concludes, "Then you're a warrior. That's what you are. Argue with anything else, but don't argue with your own nature" (SK, 320). Parry uses this interpretation of Will's nature to try to force Will to go to Lord Asriel. Will's father is neither deceiving his son nor asking him to do something evil. Parry is trying to help Will see what he has been created to do. But telling Will to not argue with his nature is an attempt to limit Will's freedom.

Whether we call them environmental factors, the fates, or one's nature, various forces do define the boundaries of human freedom. Pullman recognizes and by no means trivializes these factors, but it appears to be in his own nature to desire freedom for his characters—to allow them the liberty to make their own choices. Pullman wants people not just to be free but also to believe that they are free. Without this belief, people cannot act on whatever freedom the fates have delivered to them. If Lyra had been told about her destiny, her work would have failed. If Will had believed his nature was truly to fight, he might have left Lyra to help Lord Asriel. But of course Will did not do that.

The Freedom to Help Others

With a mentally ill mother and a father gone for most of his life, Will has been free to make his own choices since he was a small child. He is, as sociologists put it, inner-directed rather than other-directed. He does not do what other people think he should do but what he thinks he should do. So he does not go to Lord Asriel. He uses the subtle knife to help Lyra free Roger and others from the Land of the Dead. And though he does end up destroying the Authority, he does not do so in the sort of cosmic battle toward which others have been pushing him. When Will finally finds the Authority, he sees that the ancient being is frightened, confused, seemingly trapped in a crystal container and under attack by cliff-ghasts. So when he fights off the ghasts, Will opens up the crystal chamber, not to hurt the aged angel but help him. And the Authority, far from being hostile, responds with gratitude to this act of kindness.

After encountering his father's ghost in the Land of the Dead, Will defends his departure from his father's advice in the name of individual choice and human freedom. "You said I was a warrior. You told me that was my nature, and I shouldn't argue with it. Father, you were wrong," he says. "I fought because I had to. I can't choose my nature, but I can choose what I do. And I will choose, because now I'm free" (AS, 418).

But what does Will choose? Throughout the trilogy, Will chooses to help others. Occasionally, his compassion leads him into trouble. Routinely, it calls for him to sacrifice. When Will chooses to protect his mother, he must confront children that tease her and the men that come searching for information about his father. When he decides to help Lyra get her alethiometer back, he has to fight Tullio for the subtle knife. When he chooses to mend the subtle knife after he breaks it rescuing Lyra, he must go to Iorek for the forging. Will fights the harpies to help Lyra and the ghosts in the Land of the Dead. Will expresses his love of Lyra in a kiss. He breaks the subtle knife so that no more windows between worlds can be opened. This list of choices and their consequences could go on, but the broader point is this: while Will does fight, he chooses not to be a warrior. In the end he is defined, not by his courage but by his compassion. He chooses to help others.

This combination of freedom and *agapic* love is what sets Will apart from the Authority. The Authority uses every means possible to foster blind obedience and limit human freedom. He tells lies about his origin, uses his power to intimidate other beings, and creates institutions to control people's actions and thoughts. His followers developed horrific procedures such as intercision to cut the soul out of some children. Will, by contrast, exercises his freedom to help others, to ease their suffering and free them from captivity.

In Christianity, demons play the Authority's role. They are the beings that possess people, take over their wills, and force them to act in ways they would not otherwise choose to act. Demons overpower people's freedom, and their victims seem almost helpless to respond. One of the horrors of the movie *The Exorcist* is that inside the body of the girl, Regan McNeil, is a demon overpowering her soul. The girl cannot control her words or even her movements. She is possessed by the will of another, made prisoner inside her own body.

Jesus, of course, plays the opposite part. He expels demons and returns freedom to people. Jesus also asks people to follow him, and many people do: the disciples, the poor, the blind, the lame, women, and children. But others choose not to. If Christianity's primary commandment is to love, and love is doing what is good for another, then people must have the freedom of choice about how they treat others. Without freedom, there is no love.

Pullman seems to say something similar: without freedom there is no compassion. Without freedom there is no real opportunity for courage. The great evil of the Authority is his assault on freedom. Through lies and oppressive institutions, through scientific experiments and obsequious followers, the Authority is trying to strip people of their freedom. A loss of freedom does not just mean slavery. It means deforming and dehumanizing people. In Pullman's world, every person is connected to every other person, and each is connected to every part of creation. Restrictions on freedom damage each person's ability to relate to others. Those without freedom are kept from becoming fully and truly what they are meant to be: people in loving relationships. Domination damages not just the enslaved person but all of creation. In a panentheistic universe, in which Dust binds everyone and everything together into a web of mutual interdependence, everyone's freedom is violated by the violation of anyone's freedom. Wherever freedom is absent, a little less Dust is generated, since Dust is a byproduct of consciousness and free human action.

The Authority's assault on freedom, therefore, is nothing less than an assault on compassionate life. For Pullman, freedom is essential to human flourishing; there is no greater sin than restricting it. Without it, it is not possible to become fully human oneself or to engage in genuine relationships. Without freedom there can be no love. But freedom is not sufficient in and of itself. The Authority is free and has chosen to use his freedom to destroy others. Will, of course, has chosen to use his freedom to help others. Pullman's notion of freedom is freedom "to" more than freedom "from." Freedom "from" is the absence of restrictions and impositions—freedom from slavery, prison, or parental control.[4] Freedom "from" the Authority is what most people are fighting for in *His Dark Materials*. But the purpose of attaining this freedom is not to allow people to do whatever they please. Pullman's characters fight so they can choose to be kind and not cruel, so they will have the freedom to build the Republic of Heaven, to have good and true stories to tell the harpies after their lives are over, and, as we will see in the ensuing chapters, even to save God.

And the king will say to them in reply,
"Amen, I say to you, whatever you did for one of
these least brothers of mine, you did for me."

JESUS (MATTHEW 25:40)

PART THREE

Saving God

After the publication of *The Amber Spyglass,* the conservative Catholic journal *First Things* reviewed *His Dark Materials* as a whole. *First Things* is not the place one would expect to find a sympathetic ear for Pullman's atheism or his critiques of Christianity, but theirs was by no means an unappreciative review.

The article begins by stating that Pullman's grasp of childhood is more sophisticated than that of Harry Potter's creator, J. K. Rowling. It then calls Pullman's concept of the dæmon "one of the great inventions of fantastic fiction." The concluding paragraph of the review offers the sort of praise rarely lavished on Pullman by "Christian" publications:

> As is, I can fairly characterize His Dark Materials in this fashion: imagine if at the beginning of the world Satan's rebellion had been successful, that he had reigned for two thousand years, and that a messiah was necessary to conquer lust and the spirit of domination with innocence, humility, and generous love at great personal cost. Such a story is not subversive of Christianity, it is almost Christian, even if only implicitly and imperfectly. But implicit

and imperfect Christianity is often our lot in life, and Pullman has unintentionally created a marvelous depiction of many of the human ideals Christians hold dear.[1]

Given the conservative Catholic perspective of *First Things*, the trilogy does come under some criticism, too. The reviewer, Daniel P. Moloney, an associate editor of the journal, claims that Pullman has a weak notion of salvation. More specifically, Pullman hangs salvation on romantic love—the first kiss between Lyra and Will. This idea, Moloney writes, is one "only a love sick teenager" could love; it is far too facile for someone who understands "the complexities of childhood" as well as Pullman does. Moloney does admit, however, that Pullman remedies this weakness through a second (and far more Christian) salvific moment: when Will and Lyra choose the good of others over their own erotic love at the end of the book.

This claim—that Pullman's notion of salvation is too shallow—is itself shallow. The end of *The Amber Spyglass* cannot be reduced to two distinct salvific moments—one superficial and one more complex. It should be understood instead as a complicated drama of salvation in three intimately interconnected acts, all of which are linked and indispensable, and correspond to his triune vision of humanity and panentheistic understanding of the divine.

Our death is not an end if we can live on in
our children and the younger generation.

ALBERT EINSTEIN[1]

C H A P T E R

7

A PROMISED LAND OF
A DIFFERENT SORT

At the opening of *The Amber Spyglass,* Lyra is lying in a drugged stupor. Her mother, Mrs. Coulter, believing that Lyra will not trust her, keeps her daughter in a dreamy haze in order to protect her from the Church, which seeks to track her down and kill her. In this unconscious state, Lyra becomes a kind of visionary, hearing through her dreams the voice of Roger, who is lost and pleading for her to journey to the Land of the Dead and rescue him.

LYRA'S GHOSTLY VISIONS

As her mother plays a strange game of nursemaid, Lyra's mind wanders in and out of this "end of all places and the last of all worlds" (AS, 8)—a place "where no light shone from the iron-dark sky, and where a mist obscured the horizon on every side" (AS, 8). Roger, trapped in this barren wasteland, is desperate and frightened, "his face shaded and blurred like something half-forgotten" (AS, 8). He is, literally, reduced to

III

only a ghost of his former self, and he is not alone. Millions of other equally hopeless figures, many without faces, mill about in the shadows as he calls out to Lyra. And in a moment that will turn out to be prophetic, Lyra promises Roger that she will come and save him.

Once she awakens, Lyra's promise, made in the stupor of drug-induced sleep yet infused with the force of a mystical vision, drives her to obsess about journeying into the Land of the Dead to find Roger. She asks Will to help, and Will agrees, even though his father told him to go to Lord Asriel; the Gallivespians—Lord Asriel's spies—are determined to bring Will to Asriel's fortress. On Lyra's behalf, Will uses the knife to find the world of the dead, cut a doorway into it, and begin one of the trilogy's most moving sequences—the freeing of the ghosts from their captivity in the Authority's underworld.

What Lyra and Will find when they journey into the Land of the Dead is the grey, shadowy, and desolate world from Lyra's dreams, even more terrifying in reality. The only color and heat in this barren wasteland come from the lighted Gallivespians' dragonfly mounts and the still-living bodies of Lyra and Will. *People* is too strong a word for what Will and Lyra encounter when they reach the Land of the Dead. The creatures who dwell there are translucent and ethereal, nothing more than wispy recollections of human beings. They are, literally, ghosts of their former selves. Earlier, Will and Lyra reasoned that this world must hold people's ghosts, for "dæmons fade away when we die . . . and our bodies, well, they just stay in the grave and decay" (AS, 166). Upon arrival, their suspicions are confirmed: the Land of the Dead admits only one of the three aspects of human existence. Ghosts no longer possess the material bodies enjoyed by Will and Lyra, nor do they have the animating life of a dæmon. But they are not zombie-like either, as with the specter-devastated adults from Cittàgazze and the dæmon-severed children and nurses at Bolvangar. Though docile and obedient, they retain some semblance of a will and, in certain cases, memories of life before their exile into this underworld. With the Land of the Dead, Pullman has created a kind of cruel prison for people's ghosts, maintained by the mandate of the Authority himself.

What Happens When We Die?

As Lyra readies to cross the river into the Land of the Dead, the boatman who will ferry her insists that Lyra leave Pantalaimon on the shores. Lyra blanches, but she is determined to save Roger. After discovering there is no way around the ban of dæmons from the Land of the Dead, she abandons Pan on the shore, unknowingly fulfilling the witches' prophecy that, for Lyra to save the world, she must first commit a terrible betrayal. This betrayal wrenches her whole body, weakens her resolve, and leaves her alone in a way she has never before experienced. And it is not just Lyra who must forsake her beloved soul for this journey, though it is Lyra alone who must make the conscious decision to do so. As the boat makes its way across the river, Will and the Gallivespians experience similar, gut-wrenching feelings of loneliness and isolation. Their insides are ripped asunder, making them realize that they too have always had dæmons, but their dæmons were hidden inside until this moment. And though dæmons are forbidden to cross, Lyra, Will, and the Gallivespians all retain their bodies. As they wade into the Land of the Dead, the ghostly masses crowd around them, to "warm themselves at the flowing blood and the strong beating hearts" (AS, 296). Barely more substantial than a "fog," the ghosts can only speak in whispers; the presence of solid bodies nourishes them, bringing some relief to their misery. On top of this, the ghosts are constantly terrorized by the harsh cries and threats of the harpies: "great bird[s] the size of . . . vulture[s], with the face and breasts of a woman," their eyes "hateful" and "clotted with filth and slime," their mouths "caked and crusted as if [they] had vomited ancient blood again and again" (AS, 289–290).

Though Lyra journeys into the Land of the Dead with only Roger in mind, after witnessing the tragic situation of all ghosts, decides to save everyone. She asks Will to open a doorway out—an act the Gallivespians immediately realize will be a shocking defeat for the Authority, since by trapping the ghosts in this barren world, he has effectively prohibited the Dust that is their remains from returning to Dust again, so it can nourish the universe. "This will undo everything," says the Chevalier Tialys. "It's the greatest blow you could strike. The Authority will be powerless after this" (AS, 310). This insight engenders in the tiny warriors a newfound awe for Lyra and Will, and Tialys and Lady Salmakia vow to do everything in their power to assist in this task, even if it costs them their lives. But in order to free anyone, Lyra must first convince the harpies why they should allow the ghosts to leave; long ago when the Authority created the Land of the Dead, he gave the harpies "the power to see the worst in everyone" (AS, 316) and to feed off whatever remained of the fear, cruelty, and wickedness in the ghosts from their former lives. When the harpies learn of Lyra's plan, their reaction is fierce: "What will we do now," cries No-Name. "I shall tell you what we will do: from now on, we shall hold nothing back. We shall hurt and defile and tear and rend every ghost that comes through, and we shall send them mad with fear and remorse and self-hatred. This is a wasteland now; we shall make it a hell!" (AS, 316).

Unwilling to be deterred and in an effort to persuade them, first Lyra does what, until that moment, she has always done best: she tells the harpies a long string of fantastic lies and only succeeds in angering further the horrific creatures. Yet in desperation and when Lyra begins to speak the truth, from her experience, of the smells and noises of her old life in Oxford and the playful wars fought among all the children, who seemed to her now so long ago and far away, the harpies grow silent and gather to listen. It is through telling good and *true* stories that Lyra reaches the harpies, and then Tialys—the Gallivespian—negotiates a bargain with them:

> Instead of seeing only the wickedness and greed and cruelty of the ghosts that come down here, from now on you will have the right to ask all the ghosts to tell you the stories of their lives, and they will have to tell the truth about what they've seen and touched and heard and loved and known in the world. Every one of these ghosts has a story; every single one that comes down in the future will have true things to tell you about the world. And you'll have the right to hear them, and they will have to tell you. (AS, 317)

And in exchange for true stories, the harpies will have the noble task of leading the ghosts through the underworld to the opening into the world that Will shall cut, in order to release them. The harpies are pleased with this new and meaningful purpose, and so, with Lyra, Will, and the fading lights of the Gallivespians' dragonfly mounts at the lead, the creatures guide everyone on the long, dangerous, and harrowing trek along the edge of an abyss, until Will finally arrives at a place where he can cut a window into the night sky. And suddenly everyone halts. Even the ghosts begin to wonder what will happen next.

Will ghosts who exit the Land of the Dead retain a sense of self or dissolve into oblivion? Will their bodies be resurrected or has their time as flesh and blood on earth been expended? "When we leave the world of the dead, will we live again?" the ghosts ask. "Or will we vanish as our dæmons did?" (AS, 319). After consulting the alethiometer, Lyra is not able to say precisely what lies beyond this particular cut of the subtle knife, but she is confident that existence of a sort lies ahead:

> When you go out of here, all the particles that make you up will loosen and float apart, just like your dæmons did. . . . But your dæmons en't just *nothing* now; they're part of everything. All the atoms that were them, they've gone into the air and the wind and the trees and the earth and all the living things. They'll never vanish. They're just part of everything. And that's exactly what'll happen to you, I swear to you, I promise on my honor. You'll drift apart, it's true, but you'll be out in the open, part of everything alive again. (AS, 319)

Lyra says, on the one hand, that the ghosts will dissolve upon leaving the Land of the Dead. There will be no new body or dæmon waiting to greet the ghost. On the other hand, Lyra explains, in dissolving, the ghosts will not vanish or cease to be but rather live on in all creation. In response to Lyra's answer, one ghost steps forward and says with confidence, "this child has come offering us a way out and I'm going to follow her. Even if it means oblivion, friends, I'll welcome it, because it won't be nothing. We'll be alive again in a thousand blades of grass, and a million leaves" (AS, 320). To this man, though the dispersal of his particles might mean "oblivion," it is not *non*-existence but a different form of existence—an existence of relationships, an existence where one has the power to nourish the universe.

This question about the continuity of individual identity is also raised vividly by the last act of Lee Scoresby. Lee is one of the ghosts in the Land of the Dead, who, next to Roger, Lyra is most grateful to see once again. When Lee leaves the Land of the Dead, he does not immediately dissolve. Instead, he and several others, including John Parry, retain their ghostly form and enter the battle against the Authority and the specters on the side of Lord Asriel. Only after Lee's work fighting the specters is accomplished does he finally dissolve like the others. He "passed through the heavy clouds," Pullman writes, "and came out under the brilliant stars, where the atoms of his beloved dæmon, Hester, were waiting for him" (AS, 418). If Hester, or the atoms that were Hester, are waiting, is there some self that remains, even after the dissolution of these ghosts?

Pullman does not explicitly deny an enduring identity, but neither does he affirm individuality in the afterlife. Pullman seems happy to leave this matter in the form of a question, so people will focus not on their fate but on their connections to others and to the universe itself. Within a panentheistic view of the divine, it is possible to reinterpret the meaning of death. While classical notions of the individual or self teach that "the enduring self is the true locus of value, and that the death of that self is the greatest adversary" (according to Valerie Saiving, a pioneer among feminist theologians in the 1960s), if life is reinterpreted instead as a process, then death turns from adversary into yet another step in the cycle of life[2]. Upon leaving the Land of the Dead, life does not end but returns to that substance from which everyone is formed in the first place: Dust. As we are made from Dust, so we are remade after death into Dust.

Lyra's dear friend Roger is the first ghost with sufficient courage to step through the new window into the atmosphere and is perhaps the most moving and telling example of what happens after one dies and travels from this purgatory of ghosts to rise to what is, ultimately, Pullman's vision of eternal life. Upon leaving the Land of the Dead, Roger "turned to look back at Lyra and laughed in surprise as he found himself turning into the night, the starlight, the air . . . and he was gone, leaving behind such a vivid little burst of happiness that Will was reminded of the bubbles in a glass of champagne" (AS, 364). Countless other ghosts follow Roger in succession, each one ascending and dissolving into the heavens of the night sky, each one liberated from the Authority's miserable dominion, each one finally free.

THE NEW EXODUS

This vision of the afterlife seems at first to be a major departure from Christian theology. Yet the Apostle's Creed holds that Jesus descended into Hell after his death and liberated people from the snares of Satan. This liberation is almost always portrayed as the saving of worthy individuals unfairly imprisoned, much like the ghosts who awaited salvation through the descent of Lyra and Will into the Land of the Dead. As the Christian story goes, once these worthy individuals are liberated by Christ, they join the communion of saints in Heaven, much like the ghosts whose ascension reunites them with the community of all existence.

In the Christian Heaven, of course, people retain their identities (and their bodies also, albeit transformed). Pullman's ghosts, by contrast, seem to lose their individual identities as they are liberated from the shadows of death and united to the universe as a whole. Jesus describes Heaven as a wedding banquet, where everyone is gathered together, but each person remains distinct. In the *Paradiso* of his *Divine Comedy*, Dante describes heaven as the saints singing and dancing in harmony, greeting newcomers with the refrain, "oh joy, another soul to love," yet they are still individuals, too. With Pullman, however, even the cryptic comment about Hester waiting for Lee seems to imply a kind of existence where the individual, in his relationship to his former dæmon, is secondary to the relationship with the universe itself. Pullman's story seems to deviate from traditional Christianity largely in allowing the individual to merge with the whole.

So the first of Pullman's three aspects of salvation is the return of ghosts to creation, reuniting everyone with everything. Immortality is not separated from the land of the living or sequestered in the Land of the Dead. Immortality is ongoing participation in creation itself, helping the living to flourish. And since the divine is understood *as* creation, a door out of the Land of the Dead helps that portion of the person called the spirit to give back to creation, Dust—the divine. Though Pullman's notion of the afterlife is, in certain respects, in tension with traditional Christianity, it is quite consistent with Christian liberation theology, especially in its focus on a kind of exodus, on liberation in this world—*during this human history*—over liberation in the next. In the biblical Exodus, freedom comes, not to isolated individuals but to an entire nation. That nation is one people and is saved as one people. In the Exodus story, as in liberation theology, solidarity and relationships are the primary features of salvation. The panentheistic notion of God unites creation and humanity to God, so Exodus's emphasis on liberation is communal, as individuals are saved, not as individuals but in and through communities.

In what may be the most powerful section of *His Dark Materials* (when Lyra decides to free the ghosts from the Land of the Dead and, in doing so, conquers the fear inspired by her prophetic dreams about Roger, the despair of leaving Pan behind, and the terror wrought by the harpies), Lyra, with Will and the Gallivespians at her side, becomes the new Moses. She bravely leads an exodus out of the Land of the Dead, liberating the nation of ghosts from slavery under the Authority and unto the freedom of participation in all creation.

In *To Work and to Love: A Theology of Creation*, liberation theologian Dorothee Söelle argues that humanity learns its purpose in creation through the Exodus story. "In the beginning," she writes, "was liberation."[3] For Söelle, without the journey out of Egypt that freed the Israelites from oppression under Pharaoh, Jews today would not be a people and would not have been able to tell their history to future generations, including the Genesis story. As Söelle explains, "the

Exodus event precedes Jewish faith in creation."[4] Without liberation, Jews would not only be unable to tell the story of God creating the universe and everything in it, but they would be prevented from understanding and interpreting their place and purpose within it. "The cosmic order as such," Söelle explains, "without a liberation tradition does not reconcile slaves and other oppressed peoples, because it cannot empower them to free themselves."[5] After the Exodus, the Jews are charged with always remembering their liberation from slavery in Egypt by retelling and reliving the story of Exodus each year through the rituals of Passover.

Between the efforts of Will with his knife, Lyra with her alethiometer, the Gallivespians with their heroism, and the harpies with their hope for the future, they mark a new moment in Exodus history. This key event in *His Dark Materials* changes the lives and *afterlives* of all who follow thereafter, giving each life new meaning and purpose: to live in such a way as to have good and true stories to tell, so when a person dies and arrives in the Land of the Dead, she can look forward to the liberation that is eternal life: by gifting the harpies with the beauty that is the memory of her life in the world, she will become united once again with the living universe itself. Like the Jews who tell and retell the story of the Exodus each year at Passover, Lyra and Will know that after this extraordinary journey, they will have a truly salvific story to tell. As do liberation theologians, they must "spread the good news"—the gospel of eternal life—as far and wide as possible. That good news is this: if we build good and true stories out of our lives on earth, the heavenly sighs of eternal bliss and the "vivid little burst of happiness" that come with "turning into the night, the starlight, the air" awaits each and every one of us, too.

Once he drew; With one long kiss my whole soul
thro'; My lips, as sunlight drinketh dew.

ALFRED LORD TENNYSON[1]

8

THE EXQUISITE
TASTE OF KNOWING

Though the parallels to Exodus and Moses in *The Amber Spyglass* are unmistakable once acknowledged, *His Dark Materials* is most explicitly a retelling of the Fall, with Eve playing the heroine rather than the villain. By the middle of *The Subtle Knife* we learn that Lyra is to play the new Eve, the new mother of all. The Church discovers this fact through torturing witches to learn about the secret prophecy they are rumored to know, as well as through the use of a second alethiometer. When the dying witch finally admits the startling revelation, the Church officials present are terrified. The first Eve, they lament, horrified, was the cause of all sin and evil, and another disobedient Eve will surely allow more sin and evil into the world. Mrs. Coulter initially sides with the Church officials, saying that Lyra will have to be killed to "to prevent another Fall" (SK, 314). But the witches, Gyptians, and other enemies of the Church see the appearance of a new Eve as liberating. They believe that the name Eve, which means "mother of all the living," captures Lyra's true purpose: to give life back to the universe.

First the Exodus, Then the Fall

Like most Pullman interpreters, the *First Things* reviewer who felt the trilogy's notion of salvation was weak because it rested on the shaky foundation of romantic love (and not so subtly symbolized by Lyra's raising of a small, red fruit to Will's lips) missed how robust Pullman's notion of salvation really is. The erotic love that emerges between Lyra and Will is the second salvific moment in a much larger salvific arc (although it is definitely the one most publicly discussed) and far from simply a childish, romantic notion. The first two salvific moments in *His Dark Materials* follow liberation theology in the way that Exodus—*the liberation*—precedes Genesis—the *telling* of the creation of all life—and unfold in the following way. First, Lyra and Will save the ghosts of humanity by opening a door out of the Land of the Dead, and in so doing, reenact Exodus, paving the way for Lyra to take on her responsibilities, not only as the new Moses but also, as a result, the new Eve and a reinterpretation of the Fall. The Israelites needed the courage and leadership of Moses to be liberated from slavery and, in turn, gain a new vantage point on the creation story told in Genesis.

Similarly, before the Fall can be reenacted in light of a liberating God and within the historical world of *His Dark Materials,* all intelligent beings must be freed from bondage under the Authority—the "Pharaoh" of the underworld. In other words, before Lyra can become the New Eve who will reframe the creation story, she has to accept her responsibility to lead all people into freedom as the New Moses. Only after the Exodus are Lyra and Will poised to discover the power and freedom to save the body and, eventually, the Dust out of which the body is made, by expressing their love for one another. And before we can understand the third and final salvific moment in Pullman's trilogy—*saving Dust*—we must look at the significance of erotic love—how it comes about and why it is powerful enough to literally turn the tide of the Dust that is seeping out of the universe at an ever-quickening pace.[2]

The best place to witness erotic love, of course, is in the development of Lyra's relationship with Will and as it transforms from *philia* to *eros,* from friendship to erotic love between the events of *The Subtle Knife* and *The Amber Spyglass.* It is crucial to understand the changes in the two children that open the door to this "fall" into this very adult love, and important for grasping the meaning behind Lyra and Will's sexual awakening and its connection to the preservation of Dust. Though *eros* shows its face in many forms throughout the trilogy, whether in the fierce and dramatic love between Mrs. Coulter and Lord Asriel or in the intense and beautiful long-term connection between Balthamos and Baruch, it is the love of Lyra and Will that Pullman develops most fully. Through the lens of Lyra's relationship with Will, it is possible to see how, after saving the ghost inside all beings, these heroes must save the bodies of all creatures.

"FALLING" IN LOVE WILL SAVE ALL BODIES

When Mary Malone first completes her amber spyglass in the land of the *mulefa*—the device that will allow her to see Dust—she quickly discovers what has caused the problem with the seedpods that are the foundation of *mulefa* culture. The seedpods are worshipped by the *mulefa,* not only because they depend on the pods to provide wheels for their movement but also because they provide the oil that draws Dust to the *mulefa* that makes them intelligent beings. In other words, the seedpods are the *mulefa*'s connection to Dust. By looking through the spyglass, Mary realizes that the *sraf* (the *mulefa* word for Dust) is flowing horizontally, away from the land and over the sea—and most disturbingly away from the seedpod flowers it pollinates. After numerous observations, Mary realizes that Dust used to fall vertically, pollinating the upturned seedpod flowers and providing the *mulefa* community with more than enough seedpods for their survival. Since the flow of Dust changed, only horizontally facing flowers—in other words, extraordinarily rare blooms—can catch the flowing Dust and produce seedpods essential to *mulefa* survival.

Yet the implications of the redirection of the flow of Dust are catastrophic for the survival of *all* worlds and *all* intelligent beings in them, not just the *mulefa*. Though the Church believes Dust is the root of all sin, Dust is actually the source of all consciousness, responding to and encouraging freedom, intelligence, and self-awareness in creatures. The flight of Dust out of the worlds diminishes these capacities. If all Dust were to drain away, the world would become, to quote the witch Serafina Pekkala, "nothing more than interlocking machines, blind and empty of thought, feeling, life" (GC, 310). All beings would become like the zombie nurses at Bolvangar or the adults attacked by the specters. Stripped of Dust, the world and its creatures will lose their animating principle, their intelligence, freedom, and creativity, becoming lumps of matter that respond only to external stimuli in ways entirely predictable by static laws. In order to preserve everything that makes life worth living, Dust must be saved. But it can only be saved through love, more specifically through erotic love: one body learning, as the King James Version of the Bible puts it, to "know" another.

Though *His Dark Materials* explores many kinds of love, including what the Greeks call *storge, philia,* and *agape,* most important for Pullman is *eros.* Pullman demonstrates little faith in *storgic* or familial love—the love between parents and children or among siblings. Both Lyra and Will are all but abandoned by their parents, and the brief efforts at repairing their parent-child bonds are too little, too late. Both children must find alternate parental figures: for Lyra, in the Gyptians, the aeronaut Lee Scoresby, and the armored bear Iorek Byrnison; for Will, it is the Gallivespians and the angels Baruch and Balthamos who eventually come to protect him out of genuine caring.[3]

When it comes to *philial* love, or the love between friends, the most obvious example of this in the trilogy is the beginning relationship between Lyra and Will, one that burns with intensity (though initially without sexuality) from the moment of their first meeting in Cittàgazze. Shortly after Will follows the stray cat through the mysterious window under the hornbeam trees in his Oxford into Citagàzze, Lyra follows Lord Asriel across the bridge he blasted into the sky that also leads to Citagàzze. Will enters a house with a café downstairs looking for food and a place to rest, and it is here that their universe-altering first meeting takes place. As Will stands pondering his situation in this seemingly empty world, "the door burst open and something came hurtling at him like a wild beast. . . . [It was] a girl about his own age, ferocious, snarling, with ragged dirty clothes and thin bare limbs" (SK,

20). From the beginning, Lyra and Will encounter each other with a fierce passion, though during this first meeting their passion is expressed rather brutally and with utter distrust, chiefly in the form of fighting.[4]

When Will and Lyra sit down to eat together, Pullman shares Will's initial experience of Lyra as he watches her carefully from across the table:

> And all the time he was intensely aware of the girl. She was small and slight, but wiry, and she'd fought like a tiger; his fist had raised a bruise on her cheek, and she was ignoring it. Her expression was a mixture of the very young—when she first tasted the cola—and a kind of deep, sad wariness. (SK, 24)

Shortly thereafter, Pullman shares Lyra's initial perceptions of this boy she has just met and who will soon gain her trust like no one else before him. Lyra sneaks into Will's room while he sleeps and watches him:

> He was frowning and his face glistened with sweat. He was strong and stocky, not as formed as a grown man, of course, because he wasn't much older than she was, but he'd be powerful one day. How much easier if his dæmon had been visible! She wondered what its form might be, and whether it was fixed yet. Whatever its form was, it would express a nature that was savage and courteous, and unhappy. (SK, 27)

Each is immediately able to recognize sadness in the other, the weary signs of battles fought, and past experience deserving of respect. Each feels a spark of curiosity about the other as they try hard to read each other's movements and simple presence. So it is not only their mutual need and the stress of their situations that draws them into the adventure before them, but in a move fitting of Pullman, the pull of curiosity—a desire to know the other, how each got from another place to this moment—that propels them forward into this relationship that is destined to save the universe. And though each treats the other with caution during this first visit to Cittàgazze, caution soon gives way to true companionship and, by the end of *The Subtle Knife,* enduring friendship.

This meeting begins a connection between Lyra and Will that will grow to resemble the bond between human and dæmon—a relationship marked with the same sense of desperation and loss that people from Lyra's world feel when their dæmons wander too far away, that "strange tormenting when your dæmon was pulling at the link between you; part physical pain deep in the chest, part intense sadness and love" (GC, 195). In *The Golden Compass,* when Pan tests the limits of his ability to distance himself from Lyra, she becomes "angry and miserable . . . [and] . . . [t]he pain in Lyra's heart grew more and more unbearable, and a sob of longing rose in her throat" (GC, 195). As Lyra and Will journey further into the adventure ahead of them, they, too, begin to feel despair upon separation, an unbearable torment and unhappiness when one is away from the other. From the very first, this connection between boy and girl is destined to "settle" into something profoundly important and deeply intimate in its maturity, again, much the way a person's dæmon "settles" into its permanent form.

Yet there is still a long way to go between the *eros* that will eventually emerge between Lyra and Will and the *philia* sparked by this initial meeting, which, though clearly marked with passion, is most obviously characterized by distrust and suspicion. Before ecstatic or erotic love becomes possible, a strong bond of trust must be forged between them. Without trust, there can be no mutuality in love, and without utter mutuality, they cannot truly become "conscious of" or "know" the other in *eros*.[5] Before real trust is possible, Lyra and Will must become equally vulnerable to each other—a condition in their relationship that arises when they journey into the Land of the Dead.

WHY EROS NEEDS ROOM: FILLING THE SPACE LEFT BY ONE'S DÆMON

Does part of growing up and readying oneself for a grown-up, loving relationship, for establishing the trust required for one body to "know" another, require the realization that there is a gaping hole inside us—a hole that can only be filled by another person? Children are constitutionally narcissistic and largely oblivious to needs beyond those that affect them personally and immediately. Yet as we grow up, we develop empathy and begin to seek out others, not simply to fulfill our needs but to create something larger than ourselves. When we experience that mysterious transformation—from seeing ourselves as the center of the universe to suddenly feeling that center shift, groping beyond ourselves as individuals to others for fulfillment—our desires start to open up to relationships in a new way, and eventually we begin to require new things from some of these relationships. During this time many of us discover that feeling complete and fulfilled is realized and expressed through intense and combined physical and emotional intimacy with another person.[6]

In *His Dark Materials*, it is only after Lyra leaves Pan behind on the river bank and Will experiences a similar, though less literal, parting of his soul from his body in the Land of the Dead that their relationship begins to shift from philial to erotic love. Leaving Pan behind has many effects on Lyra, one of which is that she begins to know the importance of telling the truth, and, as a result, gains the heroic courage that will save all ghosts, both now and ever after. But the most important transformation concerns how she and Will come to see each other anew. Just after Lyra almost falls into the abyss that lines the Land of the Dead, No-Name the harpy swoops to her rescue, delivering the shaken Lyra into Will's desperate arms and transforming their friendship in this single moment of encounter. "He held her tight, pressing her to his chest, feeling the wild beat of her heart against his ribs," Pullman writes. "She wasn't Lyra then, and he wasn't Will; she wasn't a girl, and he wasn't a boy. They were the only two human beings in a vast gulf of death. They clung together. . . ." (AS, 360). After this moment, after they almost lose each other forever, Lyra and Will realize not only their longstanding passion for one other but also an intense need and even dependence on one other, symbolized in this instance by their clinging so tightly to each other. In this moment of intense vulnerability, Lyra and Will begin to move toward a more adult and embodied appreciation of each other. Their hug on the edge of the abyss is the first time their bodies meet in something other than fighting or play—in something larger and more emotionally and physically intimate than the friendship they had, by now, long ago established.

During their last moments in the Land of the Dead, there is yet another indication that their relationship has begun to change. Will needs to cut one last window out of the Land of the Dead into the world where Lord Asriel wages his battle and where John Parry and Lee Scoresby will have their last stand, yet Will has trouble concentrating sufficiently to make the cut. Worried that the knife will shatter again, Lyra urges Will to look at her during his next try—and he does. "In the ghost light he saw her bright hair, her firm-set mouth, her candid eyes; he felt the warmth of her breath; he caught the friendly scent of her flesh" (AS, 386–387). Here Will is unmistakably appreciating Lyra as a young woman, not just as his loyal friend. He is breathing in the "scent of her flesh" and gazing on "her candid eyes." Though leaving their dæmons by the river bank was unbearably painful, it seems that this decision allowed Lyra and Will to look to each other for that warming, reassuring presence once given them by their souls, which they now give to each other through their own bodies. It's as if both children needed to let go of a part of themselves before each could make space for a new level of relationship to emerge between them. Only after leaving their souls behind are Will and Lyra are able to make the most important discovery of all: that they are each other's soul-*mates*. And it is only together, as soul-mates, that they are able to save embodiment and all the pleasures and pains that accompany this state of being in—and made of—the universe.

THE NEW EVE AND THE NEW ADAM: SAVING EMBODIMENT THROUGH *EROS*

In Genesis, God created human beings and placed them in the Garden of Eden where work was nonexistent, food was provided for, childbirth was painless, shame was absent, and

God was a frequent visitor. Adam and Eve, the first two humans, could eat of the Tree of Life and never suffer death. There was only one commandment: do not eat of the Tree of the Knowledge of Good and Evil. God said they would be "doomed to die" if they disobeyed. In tranquil innocence, Adam and Eve lived in the garden. They were perfect for one another. God had created Eve out of Adam's rib—as the second creation story goes—and Adam recognized their compatibility by saying that Eve was "bone of my bone, flesh of my flesh" (Genesis 2:5). They were of the same matter and, as such, true and genuine companions—that is, until Eve asked Adam to disobey God by eating the forbidden fruit and Hell broke loose, quite literally, in their paradise.

Over the course of history, Eve has become synonymous with the temptress, the root cause of all the death, toil, and evil that humanity has endured after banishment from Paradise. Yet in Genesis, she is not the only disobedient soul in the Garden. As the story goes, she "gave some to her husband, who was with her, and he ate it." Adam was there all along, not saying a word, passively doing what he is told by taking the fruit from her without questioning its origins and biting into it without a thought. Though Eve has taken most of the blame, at least she contemplated her decision to eat of the fruit, while Adam simply took what he was given without much thought. After *both* Adam and Eve eat the fruit, trouble ensues. Adam and Eve hide from God, and the intimacy of the human-divine relationship is destroyed. When God asks Adam what happened, Adam blames God (and Eve): "This woman you put here told me to do it," he says. Adam has moved from calling Eve "bone of my bone, flesh of my flesh" to "this woman." Here Adam is revealed as a weak-willed, fickle man: as soon the wolves come knocking at the door, Adam throws his wife to them, and the harmony of the male-female relationship is destroyed.[7] The discord continues when God casts Adam and Eve out of the garden, separating them from the Tree of Life, cursing them: now they must endure hard labor for their survival, and childbirth is painful. The original harmony of the garden is replaced by animosity between humanity and God, men and women, humanity and creation, and even parents and children. This is what Christians define as the effects of original sin—effects all of Adam and Eve's progeny now suffer.

Yet Christianity has long held on to the importance and goodness of the body; the Christian belief in Jesus is a response to this situation: God sends the Son to save humanity from the debilitating effects of original sin, and to "resurrect" the body from a state of death.[8] At the heart of Christianity is the incarnation: God became fully human in the person of Jesus. Through this incarnation, all humanity has been united to God and saved, body and soul. Salvation is a resurrection of the body, not an escape of the soul from the body. People are given new life through Jesus' life, death, and resurrection. Jesus, to quote St. Paul, becomes the New Adam, the new father of all (1 Corinthians 15:45–49).

Pullman also emphasizes the importance of the body, but he has saved it differently. Whereas Christianity emphasizes the importance of the body by having God assume one, Pullman has saved the body by having a young woman and young man express themselves and their desires for each other through their erotic, bodily love. Another way of saying this is that Christianity believes humanity was saved through a New Adam alone, but this second moment of salvation in *His Dark Materials* is wrought by a New Adam *and* a New Eve together, turning the original Genesis story of disobedience into a resurrection story of a sort—a tale of the resurrection and salvation of the body mutually enacted by a young woman and young man together.

Pullman's retelling is also different because of his panentheistic understanding of God and the world in the trilogy. God is not a being separate from the world but part and parcel of the world, part and parcel of human beings—so intimate that it is as if the universe and God are *lovers,* and the erotic love enjoyed between creatures a tangible expression of this divine intimacy. Feminist theologian Sallie McFague expresses the ambiguity among Christians about affirming this vision: "[Christians] speak of God as love but are afraid to call God lover," she worries. "But a God who relates to all that is, not distantly and bloodlessly but intimately and passionately, is appropriately called lover."[9] True love, for McFague, the kind of love between God and God's creation, is appropriately an erotic love, because though "Love cannot be reduced to sex . . . it cannot escape it either, or if it tries, it becomes bloodless, cold, and sterile, and no longer the embrace that spins our pulsating earth, sending blood through our veins and drawing us into each other's arms."[10] In loving each other, we enact God's intimate love of creation, and in turn, love the universe and all that is in it. So in *His Dark Materials* there is no need for a new incarnation—for a single act of divine-human intimacy, as with Jesus—because the incarnation is already everywhere, and expressing divine-created intimacy is the foundation and purpose of all intelligent beings. Having an isolated individual bring about salvation would go against the grain of Pullman's universe, where everything is relational. Individuals are connected to

Dust and, through Dust, to every other being in the universe, from angel to *mulefa*. Individuals are never alone because they (almost) always have their dæmons with them, whether these dæmons are inside or outside of them. So to have an individual redeem a relational world would not work in *His Dark Materials*. It is a couple then—a loving relationship between embodied beings—that can redeem a relational world, can *save* the divine-embodied relationship. One needs a New Adam and a New Eve, and they need to be working—and loving—together.

Again, the original Eve was the mother of all people (Genesis 3:20). If Lyra is the New Eve, she must somehow bring life. Because Dust is the source of freedom, consciousness, and passion—the source of created life—Lyra must alter the pathway of Dust from out of the world back toward it, setting in motion the salvation of the animating principle of life. This is a kind of reverse resurrection: Dust does not flow up and out of the world into heaven; rather, Dust returns to its true home in the bodies and creatures of the universe. Though she does not physically give birth to children, Lyra re-opens the door to a future in which every intelligent being can truly be alive rather than being trapped in a passionless and deterministic universe like a mindless lump of matter, "bloodless, cold, and sterile," as McFague describes. In "giving birth" to this life, Lyra will have almost fulfilled the prophecy about her—that she will bring an end to destiny, which represents life *without will* (and as we will see, quite literally, without Will). Without the will, bodies become lifeless matter, subject to the forces of nature without any ability to change, respond, or adapt as if rocks, dirt, or waves. They would be "destined" to act by the laws of nature without the power or intelligence to resist or rework these laws. Dust generates the freedom of all intelligent beings, expressed through the internal forces of the will, intellect, and imagination. Human bodies do not degenerate "into machines, blind and empty of thought, feeling, life," but rather, through Dust, become bodies alive with feeling, thought, and action. Therefore, for Lyra to become the New Eve, she must do so of her own free will, through a choice of her own making.

So how does this New Eve "give life" and set in motion the salvation of Dust? How does Lyra affect this "reverse resurrection"? First and foremost, she does it by realizing her love for Will. After cutting into the world of the *mulefa*, Mary Malone finally plays her own fated role in this story: becoming the temptress. Mary Malone tells a rapt and transformed Will and Lyra the story of her first kiss and of falling in love with a man. This narrative helps Will and Lyra understand not only their mutual love but also how to act on it. After listening to Mary's stories, they kiss. Presumably, they also make love—they "become conscious," they *know* each other bodily. Yet their union is not merely sex; it is divine *eros* embodied in its most profound form, the kind of lovemaking that McFague says "express[es] the Christian vision as an inclusive one of fulfillment" and that "must be allowed its hallowed place as the one act that up and down the ladder of creation signifies the desire to be united with others."[11] Through the experience of erotic love, the relationship between Lyra and Will is fully transformed, and for a time they let go, even of their desire to be reunited with their dæmons:

> Will and Lyra went out by themselves again, speaking little, eager to be alone with each other. They looked

dazed as if some happy accident had robbed them of their wits; they moved slowly; their eyes were not focused on what they looked at. . . . They spent all day on the wide hills, and in the heat of the afternoon, they visited their gold-and-silver grove. They talked, they bathed, they ate, they kissed, they lay in a trance of happiness murmuring words whose sound was as confused as their sense, and they felt they were melting with love. (AS, 481)

Like McFague, or liberation theologian Dorothee Söelle, to be "melting with love" for another person, as Lyra and Will are with each other, is to become "erotically connected with the world."[12] For Söelle, "The ecstasy of lovemaking frees us to understand our want: how alone, how incomplete, how broken we are without participation in ecstasy. . . . The earth is a sexual planet, and we affirm its being good in celebrating the true richness of the human being in loving and in making love."[13] And the expression of bodily love through sexuality precipitates a change in us; it empowers us to participate in the creative power of God. That is why it's so ecstatic.

In Pullman's terms, what makes Lyra and Will "melt with love," what makes their connection so *ecstatic*, is not their participation in the creative power that is Dust but *Dust's* intimate participation in the creative power of their bodies. In the beginning pages of *The Amber Spyglass*, the angel Balthamos explains that "Dust is only a name for what happens when matter begins to understand itself. Matter loves matter. It seeks to know more about itself and Dust is formed" (AS, 28). When Lyra and Will seek to "know more" about each other, they literally become the image of matter loving matter, the fulfillment of Dust's desire. If Dust is made when matter begins to "know" itself, it makes sense that created beings would begin to attract Dust when their bodies discover themselves through loving other "matter," other bodies. And according to McFague, God is not only "interested" in "the entire beloved cosmos," but God finds it all exquisitely "valuable and attractive."[14] It is through *eros*, for McFague, that God and the created together enact the world's salvation.

It follows, then, that Mary Malone does not need her spyglass to see that Lyra and Will, upon returning from their first excursion into expressing the erotic love between them, "would seem to be made of living gold," as if made of Dust themselves. And the attraction of Dust to Lyra and Will's soul-uniting is so powerful that, in knowing each other's bodies for the first time,

> The terrible flood of Dust in the sky had stopped flowing. It wasn't still, by any means; Mary scanned the whole sky with the amber lens, seeing a current here, an eddy there, a vortex farther off; it was in perpetual movement, but it wasn't flowing away anymore. In fact, if anything, it was falling like snowflakes. (AS, 470)

Dust, at least for the time being, halts its progression out of the world because it has found its "living home again"; it has rediscovered the force that pulls it toward Pullman's version of heaven: intelligent, living bodies. Instead of seeping out of the gaping windows between worlds cut by the knife and the abyss along the edge of the underworld, it is irresistibly drawn to these "children-no-longer-children, saturated with love." Even the battle the Authority is waging against freedom, thought, and feeling is defeated by the love embodied by these young soul-mates. All matter and all bodies are suddenly and exquisitely bathed in Dust, as they should be—and they are saved.

The feeling remains that God is on the journey, too.

SAINT TERESA OF AVILA

9

LOVE'S DIVINE SACRIFICE

In addition to a New Moses, a New Eve, and a New Adam, Pullman's salvation story includes a New Mary, who plays a major role in the trilogy's third and final moment of salvation. While the mother of Jesus assisted Jesus in his saving work, Mary Malone helps Lyra and Will save Dust, which, in the universe of *His Dark Materials,* is tantamount to saving God.

THE GOOD SERPENT

Just as Lyra and Will play several biblical roles, however, Mary Malone's part is not restricted to playing the role of the serpent who tempts the New Eve and the New Adam into embodying their saving love for each other. In addition, this New Mary is charged with facilitating Will and Lyra's tragic goodbye at the end of *The Amber Spyglass,* a mystifying moment for many readers.

"You must play the serpent!" says Mary's Cave in *The Subtle Knife* (SK, 250).

Could Mary have known what was in store for her when particles of consciousness communicated this imperative to her through the Cave—the computer that Mary's research team developed for measuring dark matter? Mary was, after all, a former nun, and "play the serpent" sounds like a pretty miserable role, given most readings of Genesis. Of course, in *His Dark Materials,* playing the serpent takes on a very different meaning. In Pullman's retelling of this Judeo-Christian myth, God is the evil Authority. So the serpent who has traditionally been seen as evil is, in truth, a bringer of good. The serpent was telling the truth when he said that the people will "surely be like God." If they ate the fruit, Adam and Eve would move from their obedient servants of God to a position of autonomy, maturity, and freedom.

So the serpent really helps Adam and Eve and, through Eve's decision to partake of knowledge, everyone in creation becomes empowered to rebel against the tyrannical deity who tries to control and oppress them. And in *His Dark Materials,* Mary Malone is called to this good task. She is to help a New Adam and a New Eve remove themselves from the domination of the Authority. Though Pullman presents a radically alternative reading of Genesis, his version of the Fall is actually the story of Mary in traditional Christianity. In this case, however, Mary will give birth to two saviors.

MARY MALONE AS MARY THE MOTHER OF THE SAVIOR(S)

In Christianity, Mary the mother of Jesus has always held a special role. Catholics believe that she was not only assumed into heaven (The Assumption) but was also born without the stain of original sin (The Immaculate Conception). Many Catholics also attest to seeing her appear at Guadalupe, Lourdes, Fatima, and other shrines of Marian devotion. The praise bestowed on Mary comes almost entirely from her role as the mother of Jesus—a role she played with humility and obedience. When the angel Gabriel appeared to her and announced that she had been chosen to be the mother of God, Mary's response was, "Behold, I am the handmaid of the Lord. May it be done to me according to your word" (Luke 1:38). Although Mary does not bring about salvation herself, she helps to foster it by giving birth to the messiah who brings salvation. She helps Jesus grow up so that he can do what he is called to do.[1]

Often the story of Mary focuses on her agreeing to be God's mother and glosses over the rest of her relationship with Jesus. Mary agrees to help in God's plan of salvation by bearing God's Son, but this role does not come with a list of predetermined activities. In fact, Mary turns out to be far more normal than we might expect the "sinless" mother of God to be. What does it mean to raise the Son of God? Mary struggles with the implications herself. When Jesus is twelve years old and leaves her to debate the scribes in the Temple, she chastises him for being irresponsible. Jesus reminds his mother that he is here to do God's work and that she is supposed to help him (Luke 2:41–50). When Jesus and Mary are at a wedding and the hosts run out of wine, Mary urges her son to do something. Reluctantly, Jesus turns the water into wine but reminds Mary that this sort of miracle making is not really his role (John 2:1–11). Later, when Jesus has begun preaching and performing exorcisms, Mary becomes worried about what he is saying and doing, convinced that her child is now "out of his mind" (Mark 3:21).

Many Christians assume that Mary should be lauded simply because she was chosen by God or because of her willingness to submit herself to God in the service of others. Over and over again, from the first moment of her agreement to help God, Mary decides to help and help and help. She does not bring about salvation herself, but she definitely assists Jesus, who brings it about. Mary is neither docile nor obsequious when it comes to her relationship with Jesus or, for that matter, with God. Rather, she is a person who uses her mind and will to accomplish what she deems necessary. Through her many choices, she gives "birth" to the possibility of salvation and serves as the "midwife" who assists in its delivery.

Mary's role in Christian salvation is almost identical to Mary Malone's role in Pullman's notion of salvation. First and foremost, Mary Malone is called, not to save the world but to assist others in doing so. Dust, through the Cave, tells Mary that "you have been preparing for this [role as the serpent] as long as you have lived" (SK, 251). It seems to be her destiny. But the destiny—to help Will and Lyra—is not fulfilled without her own thoughts and actions. Again like Mary the mother of God, she chooses to accept her call, to bend her will in the direction of her destiny. She too comes into her role gradually, by helping others along the way.

THE THREAT OF LOSING GOD

After Mary sets out to invent a device (the amber spyglass) that becomes her telescope or magnifying glass through which she can see Dust, her *mulefa* friend Atal takes her to Sattamax, the wise *mulefa* elder. From him, Mary learns of the plight of the *mulefa*, how for three hundred years the trees had been producing fewer seed pods, how the violence of the predatorial tualapi had been increasing, and how, as a result, the *mulefa* and their way of life were in danger of dying. After Sattamax spoke of the *mulefa*'s tragedy, he paused and waited for Mary to respond. She offered to help any way she could. Only then did the elder put his trust in her, hoping that she would serve as a vehicle for saving his people:

> You can see things that we cannot, you can see
> connections and possibilities and alternatives that
> are invisible to us, just as sraf was invisible to you.
> And while we cannot see a way to survive, we hope
> that you may. We hope that you will go swiftly to the
> cause of the trees' sickness and find a cure; we hope
> you will invent a means of dealing with the tualapi,
> who are so numerous and so powerful.
>
> And we hope you can do so soon, or we shall all
> die. (AS, 234)

To help her with this task, the *mulefa* build a platform so she can stay in the trees. From this heightened perch, by using the amber spyglass she realizes very quickly what the problem is: Dust is flowing out of the world instead of dropping down onto it. Over the course of thirty-three thousand years, the seedpod flowers had evolved to face upward and catch the falling *sraf,* but because the *sraf* was now flowing horizontally out of the world, few flowers were being pollinated.

This grand challenge of helping to save the world of the *mulefa* is punctuated by a series of smaller, everyday tasks taken up equally graciously by Mary after Lyra and Will arrive. Recognizing their initial exhaustion, she does not ask them to recount their tale. Instead, she is patient, telling her own stories; most important, the stories are about her romantic life. She believes these stories will help them, even though she does not know how or why. Mary's romantic stories help Lyra and Will understand their feelings for one another. By acting on these feelings, they cause the flow of Dust to fall downward instead of hurrying out of the world. Mary, in short, helps Lyra and Will become saviors of all the worlds, including the world of the *mulefa*. She does not give Lyra and Will physical birth but gives birth to their love through her stories. In fact, this Mary is the mother, both of their sexuality and of their self-giving sacrifice.

Aside from the portrayal and death of God, the consummation of erotic love between Lyra and Will is the most controversial aspect of *His Dark Materials*. Because this consummation is most commonly understood as the ultimate salvific act in the trilogy, at first glance for many readers, their subsequent parting is not only tragic but perplexing. Why this harsh ending? Why does Pullman require of his young lovers such a painful goodbye, such a cruel cutting off of love—an *intercision* of sorts? Both of these young adults have experienced so much loss already. How can Pullman ask of them another, greater sacrifice? And how, if at all, can readers accept it?

The development of the relationship between Lyra and Will from companions to friends to what most readers regard as lovers, and their subsequent parting, is no doubt harsh; it is perhaps the most tragic storyline in the trilogy. Yet it is through this particular thread that we learn of the final salvific moment that remains in the trilogy: that although by loving each other, Lyra and Will draw Dust intimately back toward what it loves most of all, *matter,* there is more saving left to do. Dust—*the fabric of the divine*—cannot enact salvation alone. Between the abyss in the underworld and the many cuts made by the subtle knife, there are many tears in this divine fabric; God and God's relationship to creation is torn asunder, deeply wounded and in need of healing. So Dust needs Lyra and Will to love Dust so fiercely, so utterly, that they will do whatever is necessary to ensure that Dust is not only temporarily repaired but that this intimate union between Dust and creation is mended in such a way that it endures for always. Sallie McFague expresses this idea in vivid, theological terms:

> God as lover finds himself needing the help of those very ones among the beloved—of us human beings—who have been largely responsible for much of the estrangement that has occurred. We are needed lest the lover lose her beloved; we are needed so that the lover may be reunited with his beloved. The model of God as lover, then, implies that God needs us to help save the world![2]

So though the parents of Lyra (Mrs. Coulter and Lord Asriel) may take heroic leaps into a literal abyss in order to save their special child, the sacrifice of their lives pales in comparison to the sacrifice Pullman eventually asks of his New Eve and New Adam. This sacrifice begins with a choice. Either Lyra and Will stay together *or* they can save that precious substance, that animating principle of the universe—*Dust*—the very thing that sent Lyra journeying after Lord Asriel in *The*

Golden Compass in the first place and set the wheels in motion for her meeting Will. Lyra and Will, now in love with each other, are left facing the daunting task of saving God.

LOSING "LOVE" TO SAVE "LOVE"

At the start of the trilogy, when Lyra and Pantalaimon are hiding in the wardrobe, eavesdropping on her "Uncle" Asriel in the Retiring Room, Lord Asriel first reveals the photograms from the North. The scholars gasp at several, but one in particular astounds them: a photogram of a man and a child standing next to him, with the man bathed in a mysterious, glowing substance. This is the first moment of Pullman's new gospel in *His Dark Materials*. It is also our introduction—and Lyra's—to Dust. Here we first glimpse the divine principle at work in the universe and how this principle of freedom and creativity and consciousness acts in relation to intelligent beings.

Overall, Pullman's trilogy tells the story of a group of diverse and courageous individuals who work together to save the universe. But this story is also about God's desire to reveal the nature of divinity to these individuals, as well as their reciprocal desire to understand and even to save this divine principle from extinction. Dust is never more delighted than when we delight in each other's bodies—when two beings made from matter and Dust come to love one another bodily, to truly *know* each other. It is through our embodiment that Dust begins to settle on us. The more "love" we make, the more Dust there is in the universe.

As in Christianity, when God the Father asks God the Son to give up his life to save humanity, Dust asks a sacrifice of her female and male saviors, her New Eve and New Adam. In the Garden of Eden, the first Eve and the first Adam were exiled from Paradise for their misdeeds. This time, no punishment is involved, but Will and Lyra become exiles, too. For Dust to continue to inform us, for Love to live on in history, Lyra and Will must sacrifice the *eros* they have just discovered in one another. They do so, however, in order to save Dust—to save consciousness and freedom and play and thought and choice, to save, in other words, the possibility of love for others. So Lyra and Will

Give up *loving* one another to save LOVE.
Give up *knowing* each other to save KNOWLEDGE.
Give up *living* a life together to save LIFE.
Give up their own *future* to save the FUTURE.

The parting of Lyra and Will at the end of *The Amber Spyglass* is the final salvific moment in the trilogy; by saying goodbye, by healing all the wounds in the fabric of the universe, effectively sealing each off from the other, they save GOD.

But their story does not end with their parting. It just enters a new historical moment. Their story is "good news," as through it, the possibility of a Republic of Heaven on Earth is made viable—a diverse Republic, of course, because it must be built out of free will by the inhabitants of each unique world and not, as Asriel had originally envisioned, as its own world. Through this new gospel, both God's story and the story of intelligent life in the universe have new futures.

WHY GOD NEEDS SAVING

In Exodus, God reveals God's self to Moses and the Israelites, first in the burning bush and then with plagues on the Egyptian people and miracles performed on behalf of his chosen people. Many liberation theologians read Exodus as logically preceding Genesis; the Israelites have to be liberated from slavery to become a people, and only once they are a people do they ask about and remember their creation. Similarly, it is possible to read God's revelation of God's self to his chosen people as an act, not only of saving the Israelites but also of saving God. In all religions, the gods are intimately related to their worshipers, who offer them prayers and praise and, in many cases, even food and drink. Gods may sustain their believers, but believers just as surely sustain their gods, not least by remembering their names, writing down their revelations, and retelling their stories. If the Israelites had not been liberated from the yoke of the Pharaoh, if they had died away in Egypt, Yahweh's story—Yahweh's memory—would have been in jeopardy. Without the Israelites to pass on memories of their God, Yahweh may have faded into oblivion, much as many of the ancient Babylonian gods did.

In *His Dark Materials,* the saving of God is more literal than this. Although Pullman is often read as something of a Death-of-God author, his salvation story culminates, not in the death of God but in God's salvation. In the afterglow of their newfound love, Lyra and Will are faced with the harsh dilemma that Pullman's readers now know so well. In order to free the ghosts from the Land of the Dead, they have opened a door between worlds—one they decide must never be closed. Moreover, the physical expression of their erotic love has altered the flow of Dust across those worlds, so that Dust is falling down once again and bodies are no longer in danger of becoming mere automatons. Nonetheless, everyone remains in danger because Dust is still in danger. In other words, God—that animating principle necessary to the life of all intelligent beings—needs those very same beings to continue to survive.

Lyra and Will do not immediately recognize the gravity of the situation. Serafina Pekkala approaches Pantalaimon and Kirjava (Lyra's and Will's dæmons) to tell them about this problem and the cruel choice needed to address it. Pantalaimon and Kirjava have already understood the situation and, despite their own passionate protests, reckoned with the necessity of the solution. They know what has to be done. So do Mary and the angel Xaphania. So does everyone except, it seems, Will and Lyra. It takes the compassionate pleading of their dæmons to get Will and Lyra to embrace the unhappy path before them.

Unlike energy, Dust is a vulnerable sort of thing that can be created and destroyed. It is generated by thought, freedom, and passion and is lost when intelligent beings act irresponsibly against it, making wounds in creation with their greed, carelessness, and arrogance, destroyed with cuts made by the subtle knife and diminished by specters who "grow by feeding on Dust . . . and on dæmons . . . [b]ecause Dust and dæmons are sort of similar" (AS, 486). The wounds between worlds must be repaired in order to stop the loss of Dust and the destruction of dæmons. Once Will and Lyra grasp this fact, they are frozen with the cruel realization that to save all the worlds, they will need to separate. Will and Lyra struggle to find "a way through" or "a loophole." The first possibility is obvious: Will could cut between his world and Lyra's, then quickly close up the window so that very little Dust escapes. Unbeknownst to Will, though, the knife that enabled him and Lyra to retrieve the stolen alethiometer from Lord Boreal, to free ghosts from the Land of the Dead, to make their escape out of many a sticky situation (and, ironically, to meet each other) is also the source of the Dust-eating specters. Each knife cut allows a new specter to enter creation. (As Iorek Byrnison warns Will, "What you don't know is what the knife does on its own. Your intentions may be good. The knife has intentions, too" (AS, 487). Cittàgazze was filled with specters because the subtle knife had been used so often in that city. Will and Lyra cannot use the knife to cut back and forth between worlds because doing so would generate more specters and, in so doing, destroy more dæmons and more Dust.

Will and Lyra next contemplate living together in one world. Will has to return to his world to care for his mother, so perhaps Lyra could accompany him. Or perhaps Will could eventually make his way into Lyra's world. When Lyra offers to return with Will to his world, Will realizes the problem. It was the same problem his father had encountered earlier: people cannot live long in a world that is not their own. If they do not return to their own worlds, both they and their dæmons will age rapidly and die early. If Lyra lived in Will's world, she might survive into her twenties. Will would be growing strong and maturing while Lyra would be weakening and aging. They would not be able to do what they were supposed to do: spread the good news about the Republic of Heaven and tell people that it is essential to live in such a way as to have good and true stories to tell the harpies in the Land of the Dead. This crucial task would be limited to one world and, all too quickly, it would rest on Will's shoulders alone.

If cutting through worlds or living in each others' worlds is not possible, perhaps they could just leave one window open? If Will and Lyra committed to *not* creating any more windows, no additional specters would be created. If only one window is left open, very little Dust will be sucked out, and surely the kindness and helpfulness of people could easily compensate for the flow of Dust out of a single window. The angel Xaphania, who is helping to guide Will and Lyra through this thought process, initially assents to this strategy, seeing no reason why one door cannot be left open.

Yet the hope and joy that follows on this conclusion quickly collapses. One door already needs to be left open: the door out of the Land of the Dead. To leave a door open for themselves, Will and Lyra would have to once again imprison all current and future ghosts in the Land of the Dead. After seeing the hope in so many ghosts' faces, and after all the struggles Will and Lyra went through to open the door, they simply cannot seal it up again.

No more options are left. All possibilities are exhausted. Will and Lyra realize that they must separate forever. They must return to their own worlds, and every window and opening between and out of those worlds must be sealed up. There can be no more cutting by the subtle knife, which must be destroyed to prevent any future release of specters. Will and Lyra must work separately in their different worlds to build the Republic of Heaven. Xaphania empathizes with them but offers no false hope:

> Your sorrow has left traces in the air. This is no comfort, but believe me, every single being who knows of your dilemma wishes things could be otherwise; but there are fates that even the most powerful have to submit to. There is nothing I can do to help you change the way things are. (AS, 491)

This is a logical conclusion but not necessarily an emotionally viable one; as Will and Lyra are free beings (at least as long as Dust exists), they could act differently. They could neglect the call to build the Republic of Heaven and choose that one of them live in the world of the other. They could keep the knife and continue to cut from world to world, keeping themselves safe from the specters but unleashing them on others. They could seal up the exit from the Land of the Dead to preserve a window between their own worlds. Just because they know what should be done does not mean they have to do it.

Yet they choose to do what needs to be done: they choose to save Dust, to repair the fabric of the divine. They express an astoundingly intimate, erotic love for the divine. Will and Lyra make their choices, not for the satisfaction of their own desires but out of a "higher love" for all creation—on what is loving for the dead, for strangers in other worlds, for friends and family members in their own worlds, and, finally, for Dust itself, for consciousness and creativity, freedom and divinity. Lyra and Will choose to love in a way that sacrifices their own desire to be together on behalf of their larger love for all worlds. They sacrifice their own erotic love to save Erotic Love, to allow Love to flourish among others for all the future. This is, Pullman implies, the right choice, but it is no less difficult because it is right.[3]

For an atheist, Pullman has come to a surprisingly Christian conclusion. Echoing the Gospel of John, he seems to conclude that the key to the universe is love and that Real Love requires great personal sacrifice for the love of others. Jesus' mission was to save people. He came to preach and to heal but also to show God's way of self-giving love. After learning of the death of his friend John the Baptist, Jesus can see that his own path is leading to an early death also. Yet he chooses to stay on that path. Out of love, he chooses the path that will lead to human salvation. Jesus could have saved himself, but in the process he would have betrayed everything he stood for. If he had fled, he would not have attained salvation for humanity. So when the Roman soldiers show up in the Garden of Gethsemane, Jesus realizes, just as Will and Lyra conclude in their situation, that there is no way forward other than self-sacrificing Love.[4]

THE ULTIMATE LOVE AFFAIR: DUST LOVES US!

Self-sacrifice as the path to a higher salvation is a surprising conclusion in a novel that has thus far celebrated embodiment and championed the right of created beings to love whenever and whomever they so choose. The message seems to be that our allegiance should never be to any single person but to humanity or creation as a whole. Or, to put it another way, our core relationship should not be with another person but with Dust or, as we interpret it in this book, with the divine. This is of course a major theme in many of the world's religions, which urge their participants to love God first and their spouses or children second. And Pullman seems to give a resounding endorsement of this view here. If the preservation of consciousness and creativity and everything else that Dust represents requires sacrifice—even the sacrifice of erotic love, at least on a personal level—then we must be prepared to make that sacrifice, to say the goodbyes that it demands. We must love Dust or divinity or Love itself more than we love our beloved. As Hadewijch of Antwerp, the thirteenth-century woman mystic and visionary, expresses through her poetry, there is a difference between love and Love: human love is expressed with a lower-case "l" because it is of a lesser form than divine Love, which she marks always with a capital "L" to signify its greatness.[5]

Like the world of the Christian New Testament, the universe that Pullman has created in *His Dark Materials* demands bodily sacrifice, not a singular death as in the case of Jesus but the *relational* death of Lyra and Will. These young lovers can only hope to love each other at a distance—soul to soul. And since their actions allow Dust to live on throughout the universe, they can take some consolation in the fact that their love lives on in the erotic love of others, and the collective Love between Dust and creation. Nonetheless, Will and Lyra must be willing to sacrifice their ability to love each other bodily. Just as God the Father demands the sacrificial death of his only Son in the New Testament, Pullman demands the sacrificial death of Will and Lyra's embodied love in *His Dark Materials*.

The final message of Pullman's three-act salvation drama seems to be that love among human beings is less important than Love of consciousness itself. So while *His Dark Materials* is oddly Christian, it is also surprisingly Greek, indebted nearly as much to Socrates and Plato as to God the Father and God the Son. In these novels, preserving true knowledge seems to be more important than preserving true love. In the end, the mind trumps the body. Consciousness trumps matter. Divinity demands the sacrifice of humanity.

For Pullman, Paradise comes to us only when we are willing to wander beyond the garden that is our childhood—

the Eden of our innocence—and begin our sojourn in an adult world where life is complex and love is embodied. But Pullman does not allow either his heroes or his readers to linger in that Paradise for long. Dust and divinity have demands as well, complicated ones, and soon enough they require our sacrifice. In the Garden of Eden, Adam and Eve sought after knowledge; likewise, in Pullman's world, Will and Lyra value knowledge. In their case, however, upholding knowledge requires even an even greater sacrifice. While Adam and Eve are condemned to hard work and pain in childbirth, Will and Lyra are asked by the force of circumstance to give up the expression of embodied love of each other, in exchange for the realization of a more ultimate love—their Love of Dust. Whether this is good news is up to the reader to decide. But there seems to be something of a Fall, even in Pullman's Gospel.

CONCLUSION
Building the Republic of Heaven

Now I rejoice in my sufferings for your sake,

and in my flesh I am filling up what is lacking in the afflic-

tions of Christ on behalf of his body, which is the church.

ST. PAUL'S LETTER TO THE COLOSSIANS (1:24)

By the end of Pullman's massive trilogy—over twelve hundred pages of epic story and adventure—the Authority and his Regent are dead, the spirits in the Land of the Dead are freed, the plague of the specters is brought to an end, and Dust itself is saved. Will and Lyra's work is momentous and irrevocable, but it does not mean that the story is over. *The Amber Spyglass* ends with Lyra telling Pan that they are now to start building "The Republic of Heaven."

How Do We Build the Republic of Heaven?

For Pullman, creating this new Republic would not entail the implementation of some predetermined blueprint thought up in the mind of an all-powerful deity who stands apart from the world. Such a project would contradict the values of freedom, choice, and creativity that are at the heart of *His Dark Materials*. Instead, the project of building the Republic is about telling stories. The first indispensable story is the defeat of the Authority, the salvation of the every person and every universe, of Dust itself, through the different levels of erotic love experienced between Lyra and Will. It is a story that eschews manipulation, control, and deception. It rejects belief in the "old man in the sky" god but proposes a panen-theistic god in the form of Dust, who is connected to us, depends on us, helps us, and loves us. Dust does not impose its will on creation but rather calls each person to freedom, intelligence, and love. Dust does not impose a moral law con-trary to our created nature but rather calls people to adhere to principles that help everyone thrive and keep people from destroying each other and themselves. Do not hate or kill the body. Do not shut off the mind. Do not imprison the spirit. Embrace sexuality, the physical world, and other people. Be kind. Use your mind and freedom to love others.[1]

Preaching this story and the values implied by it are the first step at establishing the Republic of Heaven. People must know the kind of world they live in, tell right from wrong, and understand what has been done so that they can live well. One of the ways that Christianity communicated its story was by creating shorthand versions of it, often taking the form of creeds. A creed provides believers with key words that do not replace the story but help people to recall it. *Pilate, Mary, God the Creator, Jesus' death and resurrection, the Holy Spirit, baptism—*all are words and phrases that make their way into Christian creeds that enable people to not only recall the story of Jesus but focus on its most essential elements. One of the most common and ancient creeds is the Apostle's Creed:

> I believe in God, the Father almighty,
> creator of heaven and earth.
> I believe in Jesus Christ, God's only Son, our Lord,
> who was conceived by the Holy Spirit,

born of the Virgin Mary,
suffered under Pontius Pilate,
was crucified, died, and was buried;
he descended to the dead.
On the third day he rose again;
he ascended into heaven,
he is seated at the right hand of the Father,
and he will come again to judge the living and
    the dead.
I believe in the Holy Spirit,
the holy catholic church,
the communion of saints,
the forgiveness of sins,
the resurrection of the body,
and the life everlasting. AMEN.

Pullman would probably be hesitant about a creedal statement, given the genre's propensity to masquerade as words from a deity and then be used to exclude and oppress others. But in the sense of remembering the story of Lyra and Will's self-sacrificing love and their defeat of the Authority and attending to the important values of this story, Pullman's story could easily fit into a creed that might look something like this:

I believe in God, Dust all-permeating,
Substance of heaven and earth, of all things visible
    and invisible.
I believe in two saviors, Lyra and Will, Dust's New
    Eve and Adam,
Who were conceived in *philial* love,
Born into *erotic* love by Mary Malone,
Suffered under the Authority,

Descended in the Land of the Dead, and
On seeing the imprisoned spirits, freed them.
They returned from the underworld
And closed all the windows between worlds,
Forsaking their mutual love to save Dust.
They returned to their own worlds to build the
    Republic of Heaven.
I believe in the holiness of freedom, consciousness,
    and creativity,
The evil of control, dominance, and manipulation,
The unity of all creation,
The importance of erotic love,
The goodness of the body,
And a return to Dust after death. AMEN.

The creed should never be used to inflict blind obedience to some authoritarian distortion of the Republic of Heaven. Rather, the creed should be used to highlight important aspects of the grand story of the salvation wrought by Will and Lyra. By hearing the creed, people would know about the universe they live in, the values they should live by, and their ultimate destiny. The creed would establish the basic ground rules out of which people could build their own individual stories, worthy enough to appease the harpies and indispensable to building the Republic of Heaven.

THE INDIVIDUAL IN THE REPUBLIC OF HEAVEN

So many people seem to be searching for the meaning of life or their special role or place within it. They wait and wait for the burning bush, an earthquake, a blinding light—some sign or appearance of God to come their way. They look to discover a prophecy that surrounds them like the one that surrounds Lyra, or to be told that they have been chosen the way the knife chose Will, or that their whole life has been leading up to some task like Mary Malone's role as the serpent. What Pullman's story implies is that these grand meanings in life are made, not by the imposition of external forces but through an individual's daily choices to help others. These choices, repeated over the course of years, create for a person a meaningful life and, ultimately, contribute to the building of the Republic.

Over and over again, Will, Lyra, and Mary Malone make decisions to try and help others and, through these choices, they create and fulfill their destinies. Other characters' lives model self-giving benevolence, too. Serafina Pekkala plays a key role in helping Lyra and Will, especially when the children of Cittàgazze were trying to kill them, even though her involvement goes against the witch custom of not getting involved in the affairs of human beings. She knows that Lyra and Will need help, and in helping them, she carves out a role for herself in Pullman's grand story of salvation. Iorek agrees to mend Will's knife, even though he admits that the mending brings him doubt—"a human thing, not a bear thing"—and makes him believe that "something's wrong, something's bad" (AS, 191). Iorek's sentiments foreshadow the realization that the knife is the source of the specters. Iorek's decision to help and depart from what is comfortable for bears carves out a special place in Lyra and Will's epic. Even Lee Scoresby, who wanted nothing more than to retire in peace, decides to do everything he can to help Lyra, even sacrificing his own life. Again, Lee's part in Pullman's story of salvation is not foreordained by some external force but by his own decision to help.

All of Lyra and Will's friends make sacrifices for the purpose of saving the universe and the stuff—*Dust*—that animates it and all its creatures.

The leader of Lord Asriel's angel troops—the angel Xaphania—succinctly describes the kinds of actions needed to help build these destinies. She tells Lyra and Will that they can save wisdom and freedom

> by helping [everyone] to learn and understand about themselves and each other and the way everything works, and by showing them how to be kind instead of cruel, and patient instead of hasty, and cheerful instead of surly, and above all how to keep their minds open and free and curious. (AS, 492)

To save all of creation and every creature in it, people must know the grand story of salvation—the story of Lyra and Will—but this story alone is not enough. The story of salvation is just the impetus for people to start helping one another in small daily interactions: by teaching others and being kind, patient, and cheerful with them. It is out of these small acts of love that creation moves toward salvation and the Republic is gradually built.

NOT OUT THERE OR OVER THERE

Pullman believes destinies are made out of the daily decisions to show kindness to others and not from a deity standing outside the world. Destinies imposed from outside would limit human freedom and limit the ability of people to relate compassionately to one another. An imposition from outside is a form of tyranny, even if it is ostensibly for the good. In addition, Pullman's panentheistic Dust is not some force standing outside the universe, dictating what should and should not be done. Rather, Dust is the substance that comprises people's bodies and souls and the substance that connects everyone and everything. Destinies must come from this source, which is renewed by the compassionate relationships between people and creation. Only through Dust can the Republic of Heaven be built. Or in less dogmatic-sounding words, only by being smart, creative, kind, and loving can the world become better and tyranny be conquered.

Pullman's insight is not and should not be restricted to his trilogy. Human beings should not sit around waiting for something to happen to them. They should be kind and compassionate throughout their lives, and by doing so, they will create for themselves a meaningful life. This line of thinking is one very similar to the ideas of Jewish psychoanalyst Victor Frankl, found in his book, *Man's Search for Meaning*. Imprisoned in the concentration camps in Nazi Germany, Frankl made an interesting discovery. He found that the people who tended to survive, or at least did not give up hope of living, were those who felt that they had a meaning or purpose in life. Even those considered strong—the leaders and professionals—all gave up if they believed there was nothing left worth living for. The sickly and the weak often endured if they held on to the belief that they had not yet fulfilled their purpose in life.

Where did this meaning come from? Approaching this question from a psychoanalytical perspective, Frankl said that meaning and purpose were discovered by each individual. It might be a book that needed to be written, an idea that the world needed to hear that only that individual had, or a spouse or a child who needed help. Whatever form it took, meaning was not handed down by some deity that stood apart from the world, dictating purpose and orchestrating actions. Rather, people themselves, in thinking about their lives and relationships, found that they had something important to contribute and they needed to live in order to do so.[2]

Not only does Pullman reject the belief that the call to help others comes from some being "out there," apart from creation, but he opposes the idea that we should distance ourselves, only helping others "over there," someplace other than where we are. Wherever a person finds someone in need, there is where that person is supposed to help. In his novel *Bleak House,* Charles Dickens tells of the wonderful Mrs. Jellyby, who is so preoccupied with helping the downtrodden Africans that she forgets to feed her own children. She takes money that could be used for her children's clothes and meals and sends it to Africa, and forces the children to work and sends their wages to Africa. The children live in squalor and physical, mental, and spiritual neglect. Mrs. Jellyby seems to find it easier to "help" those far away than the people who live in her own home. The reality, of course, is that Mrs. Jellyby does not really help anyone. She gives to the African project, as it is called in the novel, for her own reputation and justifies her treatment of the children by believing she is helping them to care about others.

This neglect of the neighbor in favor of the distant stranger is reflected in a tale about Fr. Pedro Arrupe, the twenty-eighth head of the Jesuits—a Catholic religious order. The story goes that a bunch of novices (individuals who had been in the order less than two years) from the United States had planned a trip to India to work with the poor there. They had their plane tickets and itineraries ready when they consulted Fr. Arrupe about their plan. He paused after their explanation and asked, "Are there no poor in America to help?" We do not need to go somewhere far away to help others. In fact, this desire to go somewhere else is often a mask for avoiding authentic engagement with the people already in our lives and the demands that such ongoing relationships produce. Mrs. Jellyby neglected her children. The Jesuit novices spent a significant amount of money to visit another country and neglected those around them. People should give help wherever they find the need and not look for it "over there."

In part, this focus on helping people here and now is Pullman's message as well. Will and Lyra are called to save the world, and one of the requirements of doing so is that they live in their own worlds, apart from each other. Of course, one reason they must live apart is that there can be no doors between their worlds, but an even more significant reason is that their lives' new purpose is to tell people about the true nature of the Authority and Dust (the grand story of salvation) and about the harpies awaiting the good stories people tell after their death, and the requisite need to be kind (the individual story of salvation). If they do not return to their own worlds, they themselves, as well as their work of telling others, will perish. Will and Lyra's task requires them to help people where they are, not in the romantic fantasy of some distant land or in some other world but in their home world, in the places they live, and to the people they encounter.

Pullman believes that Lyra and Will's return to their own world is necessary because only by their telling of the truth will other people come to understand their own opportunity and obligation to live justly. People need to understand the evil of the Authority and be open-minded and compassionate so that they will have a story to tell the harpies when they die. Only by having more and more people live lives worthy of a story will the world change from ignorance and slavery to one of wisdom and freedom. Only then will the Republic of Heaven be established in the way it is supposed to be, not tyrannically imposed from beyond and transcending all the worlds but rising up from people helping each other in their own worlds. Although Will was quoting his father, these words could just as easily apply to Philip Pullman: "He said we have to build the Republic of Heaven where we are" (AS, 488).

A *WICKED* INTERVIEW
ABOUT *HIS DARK MATERIALS*
WITH GREGORY MAGUIRE

Gregory Maguire is not only the author of the best-selling *Wicked: The Life and Times of the Wicked Witch of the West*, but he is a founding board member and codirector of Children's Literature New England (CLNE). For twenty years, Gregory Maguire and fellow CLNE board members have led the charge to open the eyes of readers, teachers, librarians, and academics to children's literature as a critical field of intellectual reflection and dialogue. This effort has led him (on more than one occasion) into dialogue with Philip Pullman, himself, and into many a discussion about *His Dark Materials*. This particular interview with Gregory took place, quite fittingly, over tea in his wonderful office, which is truly a magical world in and of itself.

Gregory Maguire received his Ph.D. in English and American Literature from Tufts University. His work as a consultant in creative writing for children has taken him to speaking engagements across the United States and abroad. He is a founder and codirector of Children's Literature New England, Incorporated—a nonprofit educational charity established in 1987. The author of numerous books for children, Mr. Maguire is also a contributor to *Am I Blue? Coming Out from the Silence,* a collection of short stories for gay and lesbian teenagers (from www.gregorymaguire.com).

DONNA FREITAS: What do you think about Pullman's understanding of religion in *His Dark Materials?*

GREGORY MAGUIRE: One of the things that was missing for me in Pullman's books is the sense of the transcendent spiritual impulse that does not need to compare and contrast, that instead seeks to apprehend a unity where all contradictory definitions are nonetheless at home. That does not fit into the scope of his story, but I, as a religious person, missed it. I thought it would be consoling to me to find somebody, just one person, in that vast breadth of the trilogy, espouse that understanding of a spiritual way of thinking of things.

Despite this, Pullman says one thing very important: that no answer should be definitive. Every answer should lead into the next question. He might have suggested other ways to be spiritual, ways to love God or to conceive of God beyond those that have to do with institutional organization, but Pullman's primary task was to talk about institutions. It wasn't really to talk about the varieties of human religious experience, like William James. His task was to talk about the ways in which institutional religion is dangerous. That is the best value he has delivered us, and it is a significant value indeed.

D: You mentioned questions. How did Pullman express this in his story?

G: I love the fact that the book begins, in a sense, in a wardrobe, just like in *The Chronicles of Narnia*. With Lewis, the kids enter Narnia, enter the world of God, through the wardrobe. In Pullman's Oxford, you go into the front of the wardrobe, stay in it, and you come out wiser. I am sure he alluded to Lewis and the wardrobe intentionally to say there is enough to be apprehended in this world. There is enough to be apprehended by paying attention to the world in which any character finds himself. They just need to focus their attention.

D: Given his take on religion and his emphasis on questions, do you think Pullman's trilogy is largely a philosophical work or a literary work or a little bit of both?

G: Certainly, it is a literary task, and a massively successful one. I think he's only philosophical to the extent he is making a single argument in as marvelously a complicated a way as he can. I think basically the argument is not unlike what somebody else could say in the two-word button they used to wear during the Vietnam War: "Question Authority." He's making an argument through the agency of characters, the plot, and moral meaning, but basically I think that's it, and that's not a scholarly argument. That's a suggestion. That's a kind of warning.

D: What's your perspective on how Pullman's trilogy relates to our world today?

G: I did a doctoral thesis just about fifteen years ago. In it I really only had one thought that I stretched out for about 360 pages. My thought was this: fantasy written for children was a lot more likely to speak about the conditions of the world during the time it was written. That being said, I think Philip Pullman is right on the money when he puts his story in the five or seven or nine universes and says what happens in one sphere influences another. There is an interdependency and interconnectedness between all populations. You cannot take from people without beggaring them and perhaps without beggaring yourself because you are misusing power. I am not at all surprised that it is even more pertinent now than when it first came out, frighteningly so.

D: Why do you think Pullman chose children to bear the brunt of the responsibility in this trilogy? Lyra and Will have the hardest journey of all. Why children?

G: At any given moment in the history of the world, children have the hardest journey because they have the longest journey, assuming they live the full life span. They have the longest journey, so it is by nature the hardest one. Also, there is something metaphoric about their innocence. Children have not been bludgeoned by experience into making the safe choices, so they still can make the right choices. In a way, Lyra and Will are bludgeoned by experience, and they do have to make the safe choice. They have to make the safe choice for the world, and they are hardened and coarsened into sorrow by their experience such that they are no longer children by the end of the story. Is *His Dark Materials* a metaphor for growing up? It is about growing up, growing up and accepting responsibility, even if it is not only about this.

D: What is the dæmon? What does it represent?

G: Oh, it's such a gorgeous construct and like any other phenomenal fantasy ideas, once you read about it you think, "Oh, of course, this must always have been the case." Everybody always knew about this, but nobody ever wrote a story about it before. The dæmon isn't just one thing. It's not an allegory. I thought, at first, it was an allegory for maybe a guardian angel. Then I thought it was an allegory for the *anima*, the thing in us that has not been completely cultivated. None of these work precisely, and that is because a dæmon is a dæmon. It makes its own definition. It is a brilliant, a brilliant concept.

D: What would your dæmon be?

G: It's a witch. Not to make this a conversation about me, but when *Wicked* was opening on Broadway last year and the cast album was being released, there was an event in the lobby of the Gershwin Theater where the cast and I were signing cards and things for the album. There were about 350–500 people lined up to get their albums signed. About every thirteenth or fourteenth person was a young woman somewhere between the ages of fifteen and twenty-eight. Many were black, Asian, or some other race. They would burst into tears when they got to Medina Menzel who played the witch. Medina had to keep getting up and giving people hugs because these women were saying, "I recognize, I know who you are. I recognize you. I know what this story is. I know myself. I saw myself up there flying with that broom stick, saying I'm trying to do the best I can and I'm not going up there." Sometimes I was sitting and sometimes I would just remove myself and watch. I had tears in my eyes for a long time just thinking about what I had done. I got a letter from somebody who said that they had a friend who's a Pakistani woman who went to see *Wicked* and came out saying, "I've been living in the United States for six years and that is the first time I recognize myself anywhere in the United States. I am that green-skinned witch up there saying I am not going to knuckle under even if nobody understands me." What gives me such joy about this is not just giving consolation to people, which is wonderful, but courage. Who could ask to give anything more, except for people to have bread and shelter? It's because the witch is my alter ego, she is the person who is brave enough and articulate enough to do things I don't know how to do, so she really is my dæmon. She does the things. I just stay in my pretty study and write my stories, but she is out there flying. She flies, and I type.

PLOT SUMMARIES

The Golden Compass

The Golden Compass is set at Jordan College in Oxford. It is not the Oxford of this world, however, but one of the many Oxfords in one of the countless parallel worlds. There are two major differences between this parallel world and our own. First, the Church and its God, called the Authority, has almost absolute control over the world and thus colleges and universities. For example, physics is called speculative theology. Dark matter, which in our world is a part of a theory in physics touching on the stability, expansion, or contraction of our universe, is called Dust. Dust is believed to be the cause of original sin, and anyone who disagrees with this belief is a heretic.

The second difference is that every person has a dæmon. A dæmon is an animal bound to a particular person, expressing the inner life of that person externally. In other words, in this parallel world, people's souls are on the outside of their bodies and take animal form. The form they take depends on the person. Servants have dog dæmons. Scholars have toads. Rulers have tigers.

Yet this form does not settle until puberty. Something about the onset of puberty and sexual maturity defines a person and thus defines his or her dæmon. One of the reasons the Church believes that Dust is the cause of original sin is that Dust coalesces around children when their dæmon settles during puberty. Hence, Dust brings about our sexual desires, which, according to the Church in this parallel world, is the root cause of sin.

The heroine of the story, Lyra, lives at Jordan College in Oxford. Her dæmon's name is Pantalaimon—Pan for short. She is only eleven when the story begins, so her dæmon has not settled yet. She is peculiarly free in her ecclesiastically controlled and monitored world. She has no parents (so she believes), avoids the scholars who try to tutor her, and runs wild among the gardens, walkways, basements, and rooftops of Jordan College. She is the leader of the Jordan College kids—the children of the various servants who work in Jordan College; her "second in command" and close friend is Roger, one of the kitchen boys.

The Golden Compass begins with Lyra investigating the Master of Jordan College's Retiring Room—a place where no woman is supposed to be, much less a little girl. Her original intent was just to peek into the room, but she has to hide in its closet when she hears the Master coming. Spying through a crack in the closet door, she sees the Master poison a bottle of Tokay, which has been decanted for a special visitor, Lord Asriel.

Lord Asriel enters the room with his white snow-leopard dæmon. He has come to Jordan College to ask them (or command them) to give him funds for an expedition to the North, to follow the investigations of a certain Stanislaus Grumman into the reality of multiple universes. After sending the butler out for his things and reclining to enjoy the Tokay, Lyra leaps out of the closet to stop him from drinking it and thus saves his life. Lord Asriel's response is to grab her arm and question her about her presence in the room. He then tells her to get back into the closet and spy on the scholars who are about to enter the room. If she does a good job, he will not report her. Lyra agrees, not only because Lord Asriel garners such obedience but also because Asriel is her uncle and official guardian (at least that is what Lyra has been told). Lord Asriel gets the money, departs as quickly as he came, again leaving Lyra under the care of everyone (which really means no one) at Jordan College.

While Asriel is heading North and Lyra continues to play with Roger and the other servants' children, something odd is happening across England: children are going missing. These children are not the children of the rich but the children of poor parents, the children of Gyptians (think gypsies), servants, and rural townsfolk—children who will not be missed by the more affluent and powerful of society. They are rumored to have been taken by Gobblers.

One day, Roger seems to have disappeared. Lyra spends all day looking for her friend, rallying her followers to extend the search. At first Lyra thinks of it as a sort of game, but, by the end of the day, she returns to the College, terrified that the Gobblers have taken Roger. She tries to convince the servants that Roger is missing, but the servants are set on getting her ready for a special dinner.

At the dinner, Lyra meets several dull female scholars and one enchanting woman—Mrs. Coulter. Mrs. Coulter, whose dæmon is a hypnotizing golden monkey, is beautiful, graceful, witty, and intelligent. Lyra is so captivated that when Mrs. Coulter invites her to leave Jordan College and become her assistant, Lyra temporarily forgets Roger and agrees to leave early the next morning. Before she does so, however, a servant wakes her before dawn and rushes her to the Master of Jordan College. He says he cannot stop her from going but he can give her an alethiometer, which looks like a golden compass. It has hands, but instead of directional notation has miniature images—images like an ant and a baby and an anchor. The Master tells her only six were ever made and it would be best to keep it secret, even from Mrs. Coulter. Lyra cannot make sense of the compass or the Master's behavior but does her best to hide the alethiometer before she leaves with Mrs. Coulter.

Lyra finds Mrs. Coulter's world fascinating, at least for a few months. Lyra is taught how to talk, how to dress, and how to show respect. Mrs. Coulter takes her to dinner parties and meetings and teaches her, intermittently, some geography and mathematics. Lyra's enjoyment of this social life soon dwindles, and by the time of Mrs. Coulter's cocktail party, Lyra is ready to leave and begin searching for Roger again.

At the party, however, Lyra hears someone talking of Gobblers and stops to eavesdrop. She finds out that the Gobblers are, in fact, the ones responsible for kidnapping the children, only that "Gobblers" is an acronym for the General Oblation Board, an office of the Church. The charge of the board is to stop the effects of original sin. The General Oblation Board, thus, kidnaps children, ships them North to an arctic base, and experiments on them. What is worst of all for Lyra is that Mrs. Coulter is in charge of the Gobblers.

Lyra quietly sneaks out of the party to escape from Mrs. Coulter. She is rescued by the Gyptians. These water-faring people live on and work out of their boats. They have been hit especially hard by the Gobblers. These Gyptians are gathering with other Gyptians to form a group to head North and rescue their children. Lord Faa is the leader of the rescue party and reluctantly agrees to allow Lyra to come, placing her under the tutelage of Farder Coram.

As the expedition makes its way North, Lyra starts to figure out how to read the alethiometer and get an answer to any question she puts to it. She becomes so adept at it that she helps Farder Coram send a message to his witch friend Serafina Pekkala, enables the Gyptians to contract an armored polar bear (a *panserbjørne,* one of the most feared mercenaries in Lyra's world) named Iorek Byrnison, and a Texas aeronaut named Lee Scoresby. In fact, the witches' Consul who contacted Serafina Pekkala for Farder Coram recognizes that Lyra's talent for reading the alethiometer reveals that she is the subject of the witches' prophecy about a person who will save everyone from death.

The Gyptians outfit themselves with sleds, dogs, and skins for the final leg of their journey North. As they are traveling, however, they are attacked, and Lyra is taken from the Gyptians. She is taken to Bolvangar, the General Oblation Board's compound in the arctic. Lyra pretends to be a dim-witted girl, all the while trying to figure out what is going on in the compound and how to escape.

What Lyra discovers is that the scientists at Bolvangar cut the bond connecting dæmon and child. It is a practice called intercision, and the experiments are attempts to keep the person alive after the operation. Once a person's dæmon has been removed, Dust does not settle on them and they become placid, hollow people, with no feelings or drives, no interest in sexuality, and no capability of sin. The Church sanctions these experiments of the General Oblation Board because they stop the effects of original sin.

While in the compound, Lyra finds Roger and, with Roger, concocts a plan for escaping, telling the children to leave the compound when the fire alarm is pulled. She answers their doubts by telling the children about intercision and saying that her friends are coming. When the time comes, Lyra pulls the alarm and leads the children out of Bolvangar, into the winter storm and, eventually, into the arms of the Gyptians.

Lyra, however, does not stop with the rescue of Roger. Uncle Asriel has been imprisoned on Svalbard, the kingdom of the *panserbjørne*. Lyra, with Roger in tow, eventually finds Asriel's prison—a plush, glass mansion on the top of a mountain. Asriel's imprisonment is actually an opportunity to continue his experiments on the existence of other worlds. Lyra learns that Asriel is her father (not her father's uncle, as she had thought); she also learns that Mrs. Coulter is her mother and that Asriel is bent on destroying Dust.

When Lyra wakes up the following morning, Asriel has taken Roger. Lyra tracks her father down, only to witness him cutting Roger's dæmon away from him. Whereas the machines in Bolvangar tried to keep the person alive during intercision, Asriel's machine was meant to harness and direct the energy released by the separation. It releases a blast into the heavens that rips them apart, opens up a bridge between the multiple worlds, and kills Roger and his dæmon. Asriel leaves the body behind and disappears across the bridge into another world. Lyra pursues her father in an attempt to save Dust.

THE SUBTLE KNIFE

The Subtle Knife begins with Will Parry, who inhabits the Oxford of our own world. Will's mother suffers from a mental illness, and his father, John Parry, disappeared several years earlier on an expedition to the North. Will is left to take care of himself and his mom, which he is able to do until two men in dark suits start showing up at their house and questioning his mom about his father.

Will hides his mother at his piano teacher's house and returns home to try and find his father's letters before the strange men do. Will does find the letters, hidden in the upstairs of his house, but does so just as the men are walking up the stairs. Will, knowing that he will be trapped if he stays upstairs, bolts out of the room where he found the letters and bowls over one of the men, knocking him down the stairs and killing him. Will is out the door and down the street before the other man can figure out what is going on.

Will finds the most peculiar hiding place: a window into another world. Will steps through into Cittàgazze. This once majestic town has now fallen into disrepair and is inhabited only by a few children. While Will searches for a place to rest, he opens a door only to be attacked by a girl and her dæmon. The girl is Lyra. Quickly, they make their peace with each other and discover that they are from different worlds. After conversing with a few of the children who wander through the streets of Cittàgazze, Will and Lyra learn that the city is full of specters who suck the souls out of adults, leaving them alive but without the will to think or move. The specters, however, cannot be seen by the children; actually, the specters are not interested in children before they hit puberty. As the adults flee the specters, the children are left behind and the city crumbles.

Will and Lyra use Cittàgazze as a hiding place, but both need to return to Will's world—Lyra to find out about Dust and Will to find out about his father. Lyra goes to Oxford and, following the direction of the alethiometer, makes her way to a scientist named Mary Malone. Mary, a former nun, studies dark matter—or she did study dark matter; her funding for the project is about to be pulled. Mary developed a computer device called the Cave to measure dark matter, but what she concluded was that dark matter was conscience. Such a conclusion was so absurd for a physicist that her funding was cut.

When Lyra comes to Mary's office, Mary is so discombobulated by her conclusions and her funding situation that she readily talks to Lyra about her problems and her work, not realizing the oddity of the situation. Mary even lets Lyra take a turn in the Cave. Lyra discovers that dark matter in Mary and Will's world is Dust in her world. Mary's Cave is a device like the alethiometer, in that it enables people to communicate with Dust. Mary's Cave, however, only works in symbols, so Lyra (at the prompting of Dust) tells Mary to rework her program so that Dust can communicate with Mary through words. Mary says she will do the work but asks that Lyra return the next day.

While Lyra is learning about Dust, Will is learning about his father. By calling the family lawyer, looking up newspaper articles, and reading John Parry's last letters, Will realizes that his father was looking for a reported window in the North that led into another world—a window like the one into Cittàgazze. If this is the case, Will's father could still be alive and just stuck in some other world.

When Lyra returns to Mary Malone the following day, she is chased by the police and rescued by a man named Sir Charles Latrom. Lyra is thankful for Sir Charles's help until she realizes he has stolen her alethiometer. She gets Will and returns to his house to ask for it back; Sir Charles says he will return it to Lyra if Will brings him the subtle knife from the *Torre deglie Angeli* (the Tower of Angels) in Cittàgazze.

Lyra and Will make their way to the tower. They find an old man, Giacomo Paradisi, tied up and a younger man, Tullio, wielding the knife. Will is forced to fight for the knife, and although he wins and gets the knife, Will loses two fingers. When they free Giacomo, he tells them that the loss of fingers indicates that Will is the knife bearer; the knife has chosen him as its new owner. Giacomo is the former knife bearer and shows Will what the knife can do: cut windows between worlds! Giacomo also tells Will that he must close all the windows he opens. The specters, Giacomo believes, entered Cittàgazze from other worlds through the windows left open. Once Will figures out the knife, he uses it to cut a window between Cittàgazze and Sir Charles's house and steal the alethiometer back.

Meanwhile, Lyra's friends, Serafina Pekkala and Lee Scoresby, have also been at work. As a witch queen, Serafina has taken a bunch of her witch kin to find and help Lyra. Lee Scoresby has set out to find Stanislaus Grumman. Lee believes Grumman knows something about the multiple universes that can help Lyra and the witches.

Lee eventually finds Grumman, who lives among the Tartars as a shaman. He is also known as Jopari and as John Parry. He is Will's father, who stumbled into Lee and Lyra's world through a window in his own. Grumman says that he needs Lee to use his balloon to help him find the knife bearer and send him to Lord Asriel, who is building a massive army to fight against the Authority and his dominions. Lee agrees on John Parry's assurance that it will help Lyra.

Lee flies John Parry up but is pursued by the zeppelins of the Church. Lee, with the help of the shaman, even flies into a different world, but the zeppelins continue their pursuit. Lee lands and sends John Parry through a mountain pass while staying behind to block the pass for the Church officials.

While Lee is helping John, the witches have found Lyra and Will and have helped them both. The children of Cittàgazze are after them because they have the knife—the one object that can kill specters. The witches come to rescue Lyra and Will and take them away from the city and up a hill, safe, so they think, at last.

That evening, though, Will cannot sleep. He wanders up the hill in the dark to think but instead runs into a stranger. He wrestles with the stranger but is too tired to do it for long. He finally gives in. The stranger then feels his hand for this missing finger and tells him since he is the knife bearer—the wielder of æsahættr—the God-destroyer, he must go to Lord Asriel and fight against the Authority. Then the stranger strikes a match to look at Will, and at that moment Will realizes that the stranger is his father, John Parry, and John realizes that the knife bearer is his son, Will.

Immediately after this joyous moment, Will's elation is destroyed. A witch shoots and kills John Parry because he had rejected her. Will's father is dead. Will returns to the camp in a stupor from the loss, only to find that the camp has been ransacked and the witches are dead or missing, and Lyra is gone. Two angels take charge of Will and direct him away from the camp.

Mary Malone, still reeling from Lyra's visit, changes the computer program so that it can work in words. Dust, through the computer, tells Mary that she is to leave her world and help Lyra by "playing the serpent." She is told to go to a window that will lead her to another world, but, before she goes, must destroy her equipment so no one can follow her. Mary does as she is told, leaving her world and going through the same window that Will went through at the beginning of the story.

THE AMBER SPYGLASS

The Amber Spyglass begins with Lyra being held captive and unconscious in a cave by Mrs. Coulter, who had kidnapped Lyra from the camp while Will was talking with his father. She brought Lyra to a hiding spot in a different world in order to protect her from the Church. The Church had discovered more about the witches' prophecy. Lyra was to be a New Eve, giving life to all. The Church, however, in hearing about a New Eve, worried about a New Fall and thus set out to kill this New Eve: no Eve, no Fall. While Lyra is in her drugged sleep, she hears and talks to Roger—her dead friend from Jordan College, killed at the end of *The Subtle Knife*. Roger asks her to come and help him.

Lyra's location is not hidden for long. The Church and Lord Asriel's forces both have their own alethiometers and use them to find the location of Lyra. Will, with the help of his angel companions Baruch and Balthamos, discovers Lyra's location. As he makes his way toward Lyra and her cave, Will encounters Iorek Byrnison. The two become close companions and set out to rescue Lyra together.

Lyra wakes up as all three forces converge on Mrs. Coulter's hideout simultaneously. Lord Asriel's forces and the Church's forces are battling each other outside the cave. Will is able to cut into the cave using his knife, but, when he tries to cut his way out, he is temporarily distracted by Mrs. Coulter, and the knife breaks. They are trapped in the cave.

As Lord Asriel's forces occupy the Church's forces, two of Asriel's Gallivespian spies, Tialys and Salmakia, make their way into the cave. Gallivespians are a small people who ride birds and dragonflies and whose defense is sharp poison spurs coming out of their heels. These Gallivespians immobilize Mrs. Coulter and her golden monkey, enabling Will and Lyra, along with Iorek and Will, to flee out a window that Will had left open; they escape the Church but not Asriel's spies. The forces of Asriel capture Mrs. Coulter.

The Church, and more specifically the Consistorial Court, an office of the Church, are not deterred by Lyra's escape. They have not only deployed an assassin, Father Gomez, to find and kill Lyra but also, taking the technology used at Bolvangar, harnessed the energy released during intercision and made a bomb that can kill a person in any world.

In the meantime, Mary Malone makes her way into Cittàgazze and out of it through another window. She finds herself in the land of the *mulefa,* who are creatures with a very distinctive evolution. In a world with circular-shaped seedpods from massive trees and natural stone roads, the *mulefa* developed appendages that use the seedpods like wheels and other limbs to accelerate and brake. The *mulefa* talk by using language and their elephant-like trunk to nuance the language with signs.

Mary quickly makes friends with the *mulefa* and quickly learns their culture and some of their language. What she finds out, though, is that something is wrong in their world. The trees are not producing seedpods, and, without the seedpods, the *mulefa*'s way of life will soon fade.

The *mulefa* ask Mary to help. Through a variety of experiments, Mary develops a spyglass whose lenses are covered in a type of amber that enables her to see the world of the *mulefa* differently. Mary is able to see the Dust moving and swirling about in the land—the Dust that should be raining down from heaven and fertilizing the flowers that produce the seedpods but instead is coursing horizontally out of the world. Mary has realized the problem: the Dust is supposed to fertilize the flowers but, as it is flowing horizontally and not vertically, it is not. She still does not know what to do about it, however.

While Mary continues to think about the problems of the *mulefa,* Lyra tells Will about Roger and about how she promised to help him. Lyra asks the alethiometer how they can help the dead, and the alethiometer says that they must use the knife to cut their way into the Land of the Dead. Will then asks Iorek to mend the broken knife. Iorek does it, reluctantly, because he is afraid of what the knife does on its own, apart from Will's intentions.

Will and Lyra set off for the Land of the Dead, cutting their way into the world. Will and Lyra first come upon the suburbs of the dead, which has the feel of a concentration camp: gray, hollow, empty people wandering around without direction. Lyra and Will find the ferryman to make their way across the lake and into the Land of the Dead. There is only one hesitation: Lyra must leave Pan behind on the shore. When the others ask why only Lyra, the ferryman answers that Will's and the Gallivespians' dæmons are inside them and will be pulled out as they cross the river. Everyone agrees, realizing that after they depart the Land of the Dead, they will have to go in search of their dæmons.

Like the Suburbs, the Land of the Dead is a dismal place. It is governed by harpies who relish making people continually relive the misery and sorrow in the lives. The countless multitudes of people are not people at all but only ghosts and shadows of people. The Land of the Dead was supposed to be the Promised Land for those faithful to the Authority but instead is a wasteland.

Lyra and Will set out to help Roger but soon feel as if they must help everyone. Will tries to cut a window out of the Land of the Dead but cannot. The harpies discover what they are doing and attempt to thwart them until Lyra speaks with them. Lyra says that if the harpies take them to a place where Will can cut through, then the harpies' new job will be to lead people to this exit but only if the people have led a life worthy of a good and true story. The harpies agree and take Will and Lyra to the exit.

While they are on their way to the exit, the Consistorial Court sets off their bomb to kill Lyra, with their leader, Father MacPhail, sacrificing himself through intercision to detonate it. The explosion misses Lyra but opens a huge gap, not only in the Land of the Dead but across several worlds. The abyss begins to suck more and more Dust out of the universe, doing to a much greater degree what Lord Asriel's small explosion did at the end of *The Subtle Knife*.

After trudging their way on the cleft alongside the void, Will and Lyra, with the countless ghosts from the Land of the Dead behind them, come to the place where a window can be opened. They cut open a door. The first to exit is Roger. He steps out into the new world, turns back to Lyra, smiles, and dissolves into the air.

As the ghosts make their way out, the ghosts of John Parry and Lee Scoresby stop to talk with Lyra and Will. John Parry tells them that he is taking an army of the ghosts to go fight on the side of Lord Asriel against the specters. Will opens a door for them, and they enter the battle between the forces of Asriel and the forces of the Authority, led by the Regent. Will and Lyra follow, looking for their dæmons.

The Regent has been given control of the forces of the Authority because the Authority has become an aged and senile being. He is kept from dissolving only because he is imprisoned in a glass container, preventing any force from dissolving him. When Will and Lyra come upon the Authority, his escape party is under attack from cliff-ghasts. They killed the Authority's guards and are attempting to access the glass container. Will scares off the ghasts with his knife and then, seeing the fear on the Authority's decrepit face, cuts open the container to comfort the creature. The Authority, in apparent gratitude, leaves his glass and dissolves in the air.

Will and Lyra pursue their dæmons in the midst of the battle, only escaping from the specters (whom they can now see) with the help of the ghosts of Lee Scoresby and John Parry. The dæmons finally flee the battle, into a tranquil world. Will and Lyra follow, not knowing that this new world is the world of the *mulefa*.

While the Consistorial Court's bomb failed, Father Gomez, the assassin, is still making progress. He has tracked down "the serpent"—Mary Malone—in the world of the *mulefa* and waits for Lyra to appear. Mary is unaware of Father Gomez's presence, so when Will and Lyra emerge from the battle into her new world, she welcomes them calmly. Mary realizes that her role as "the serpent" and saving the *mulefa* are connected, even if she does not know exactly how. She gets new clothes for Will and Lyra, lets them sleep, and gets them fed. When they emerge rejuvenated, Mary tells them her story. She was a nun and a physicist. Once at a physics conference, she ate a piece of marzipan and remembered what it was like to be in love. When she was young, a boy gave her a piece of fruit to eat, and she fell in love with him when his fingers touched her lips. She desired this experience again, wondered what good it did to be a nun and not have these experiences, realized it did no good, and thereby lost her faith.

Mary's story is how she fulfills her role as "the serpent" and thus helps to save the world of the *mulefa*. The story enables Will and Lyra to not only realize that they love each other but to act on this impulse. They are left alone to embrace and kiss each other. Father Gomez spies them but, before he can act, Will's angel companion Balthamos drags Father Gomez over a cliff and saves Will and Lyra.

After some time alone, the two return to the village, where Mary realizes, even without the help of her amber spyglass, that the children are now adults, covered in Dust, and that because of the physical expression of their love, Dust has started falling downward again.

Awash in their newfound love, Will and Lyra enjoy some time together before the angel Xaphania comes to visit them. She explains that the Authority and his forces have been defeated (even if they have not been vanquished) and that Dust has returned to its normal flow. The only item remaining is to close up all the gaps and windows between the worlds to keep Dust from seeping out. The shock to Will and Lyra is the realization that they must each return to their own world to live (a person cannot live long in another world), and if all the openings between the worlds are closed up, they will never be able to visit each other. They momentarily have hope when the angel Xaphania says that one window might be left open, but this hope quickly dissipates when they realize that the window out of the Land of the Dead is the one that needs to be kept open.

Will and Lyra are heartbroken. Their dæmons, who returned to them shortly before Xaphania came, try to comfort them but know that they cannot be comforted. They realize that they must return to their own world and push freedom, thinking, and kindness—activities that generate Dust—and that they must do this apart. They must live lives worthy of a good story to tell the harpies and must tell others to do the same. They know what they must do, but the departure is still heart wrenching.

Will leaves, and Mary, who is also from Will's world, agrees to help him and his mother out. Lyra returns to her own world to begin school and start building a place where truth, freedom, creativity, and honesty flourish. Lyra sets out to build, not the Kingdom of Heaven but the Republic of Heaven.

ACKNOWLEDGMENTS

We are indebted to many people for their help, brainstorming, support, cheerleading, and overall intellectual greatness in the process of working on this project, but none more so than the following individuals: Julianna Gustafson and Catherine Craddock at Jossey-Bass for their incredible editing skills, sense of humor, and patience, and Miriam Altshuler for being the best agent *ever.*

And then there's the man himself, Philip Pullman, for writing a fantasy trilogy that not only thrills us as readers but is a religion scholar's dream to think about.

Jason King: In writing a book, it is impossible to thank all the people who should be thanked. Among the many who helped me out were two excellent research assistants: Jennifer Ghesquire and Amanda Conway. They hunted down articles, transcribed interviews, and performed countless menial tasks that freed me up to work.

My students are always a huge motivation. Their work and interest pushed me to do books like this one. Thank you Connie, Sandi, Mike, and Rachel from Lourdes College and Matt, Amanda, Kim, Kris, Katie, and Bridget at St. Vincent College.

Colleagues are indispensable. Geof Grubb, Richard Gaillardetz, Fr. Jim Bacik, and Pat Odey-Murray helped me to hone my thinking and had faith in my abilities. Shannon

Schrein stands apart as one of my greatest helps and supporters.

At Saint Vincent College, Fr. Rene (my dean) and Fr. Tom (my chair) have been particularly supportive, giving me a course release to finish the book in the Fall of 2006.

Donna's initiative, talent, and ability make me a better scholar and writer. For this, for the joy of working together on another book, and for our friendship, I am forever indebted.

My parents' love and support cannot be underestimated and neither can the enthusiasm of my brother and his wife. The interest and enthusiasm of my in-laws—Paul, Florence, Mary, Don, Paul, and Kerry—was indispensable.

The love of my children kept me going when I felt like quitting.

I cannot say enough about my wife, Kelly. Her love sustained me through the writing, her mind helped me to sharpen my thinking, and her enjoyment of fantasy novels enriched all of my work on the project. For these reasons and for the enumerable other graces that come through her, I dedicated this book to her.

Donna Freitas: Last book, I thanked everyone and everything but the sun and the moon so this time I'll be brief(er).

I could not have finished this project without the advice, support, conversation, thoughtful guidance, and feedback from my friends at Boston University: Stephen Prothero, Peter Hawkins, and Christine Hutchinson-Jones.

Thank you to all the wonderful friends in my life who put up with my crazy-professor persona when I am working on a book (which is always lately, isn't it?), to my students at St.

Michael's College for being such inspirations and cheerleaders for the sort of stuff I like to write (I will miss you), to all my amazing professors from Georgetown and Catholic U, and to Gregory Maguire for such a fun conversation about dæmons and the like.

Jason—here we are again together! Imagine that. We are going on a decade of friendship, intellectual meandering, theological reflecting, and being a writing team. Your clear thinking astounds me, and I look forward to continuing in our shared path of fantasy-book geekdom.

To Josh, my husband, for being there as always.

And last, but not least, there are my parents. Thank you Dad, for pushing forward through all the hard stuff and for being forever proud of me.

And Mom, you've lived your story in our world. I like to imagine that you, too, became a "vivid little burst of happiness" like Pullman's ghosts, "turning into the night, the starlight, the air," in a sigh of eternal bliss.

NOTES

Introduction

1. C. S. Lewis, *The Great Divorce*. San Francisco: HarperSan-Francisco, 2001, 82.

2. From Laura Miller, "Far from Narnia: Philip Pullman's Secular Fantasy for Children." *New Yorker*, accessed through newyorker.com on Apr. 3, 2006.

3. Gregory Maguire, "Featured Review: The Amber Spyglass," *The Horn Book*, Nov./Dec. 2000, 736.

4. According to Umberto Eco, baroque art "never allows a privileged, definitive frontal view; rather, it induces the spectator to shift his position continuously in order to see the work in constantly new aspects, as if it were in a state of perpetual transformation." It requires the viewer to respond to it "as a potential mystery to be solved, a role to fulfill, a stimulus to quicken his imagination" (Umberto Eco, "The Politics of the Open Work," *The Open Work*, trans. Anna Cancogni. Cambridge, Mass.: Harvard University Press, 1989, 7).

5. Philip Pullman's *His Dark Materials* raises so many "magnificent questions," it deserves to be reckoned a cultural classic. In *Truth and Method*, German philosopher Hans-Georg Gadamer says that the classic endures because it evokes "a timeless present that is contemporaneous with every other present" and that "the duration of a [classic's] power to speak directly is fundamentally unlimited" (Hans-Georg Gadamer, *Truth*

and Method, trans. Joel Weinsheimer and Donald G. Marchall. New York: Continuum, 1993, 288–290). The theologian and philosopher of religion David Tracy defines classics as "those texts that bear an excess and permanence of meaning, yet always resist definitive interpretation" (David Tracy, *Plurality and Ambiguity: Hermeneutics, Religion, Hope.* Chicago: University of Chicago Press, 1994, 12). His *Dark Materials* does all this, offering readers a narrative endlessly erupting in possibilities, not only for general readers but also to scientists, psychologists, literary critics, political theorists, philosophers, and theologians.

6. Booklore, "The Big Read"; available at http://www .booklore.co.uk/TheBigRead/br_main.htm (accessed Jan. 2, 2007).

7. Bridge To The Stars.Net, "The Big Read Transcript"; available at http://www.bridgetothestars.net/index.php? p=bigreadtranscript (accessed Jan. 3, 2007).

8. William Flesch, "Childish Things," *The Boston Globe,* June 13, 2004; see also http://www.boston.com/news/globe/ideas/articles /2004/06/13/childish_things (accessed June 18, 2006).

9. Michael Chabon, "Dust & Daemons," *The New York Review of Books,* Mar. 25, 2004, 51(5), 26.

10. In an essay called "Romantic Scholarship," Michael Dirda writes, "Almost everyone who reads looks back fondly on early adolescence as the Golden Age, when books really were magic casements opening on faery lands forlorn. Back then entire afternoons might slip by unnoticed as we journeyed to the center of the earth

and around the world in eighty days." As we grow up, Dirda continues, that childlike ability to lose ourselves in books diminishes: "Those days are past, and all their dizzying raptures. Now we snatch a few minutes on the subway to peer at computer manuals, law texts, self-help guides, book-club main selections. The old enchantment is harder and harder to rediscover." Dirda's personal views on why enchantment on the page becomes rarer or less passionate as we become older is that there is an absence of wonder in adult reading—a wonder that animates Pullman's trilogy. Dirda explains: "Too many of our books feel middle-aged—stale, desperate, flat, tricked out in gaudy colors but tired and jaded inside. Is there any escape from such humdrummery?" (Michael Dirda, "Romantic Scholarship," *Readings: Essays and Literary Entertainments*. New York: Norton, 2000, 38).

11. There are already many books published about *His Dark Materials*. Among the more notable are the following: Mary Gribbin and John Gribbin, *The Science of Philip Pullman's* His Dark Materials (New York: Knopf, 2005); Millicent Lenz and Carole Scott, *His Dark Materials Illuminated: Critical Essays on Philip Pullman's Trilogy* (Detroit, Mich.: Wayne State University Press, 2005); Tony Watkins, *Dark Matter: Shedding Light on Philip Pullman's Trilogy* His Dark Materials (Downers Grove, Ill.: Intervarsity Press, 2004). There are also a number of significant, critical journal articles and book chapters about Pullman and his work, including: Anne-Marie Bird, " 'Without Contraries Is No Progression': Dust as an

All-Inclusive Multifunctional Metaphor in Philip Pullman's 'His Dark Materials,'" *Children's Literature in Education,* 2001, *32*(2), 111–123; Beppie Keane, "Of the Postmodernists' Party Without Knowing It: Philip Pullman, Hypermorality, and Metanarratives," *Explorations into Children's Literature,* Mar. 2005, *15,* 50–59; David R. Loy and Linda Goodhew, "The Dharma of Death and Life: Philip Pullman's *His Dark Materials* and Ursula K. Le Guine's *Earthsea.*" In *The Dharma of Dragons and Dæmons: Buddhist Themes in Modern Fantasy*" (Boston: Wisdom Publications, 2004, 101–144); Millicent Lenz, "Story as a Bridge to Transformation: The Way Beyond Death in Philip Pullman's *The Amber Spyglass,*" *Children's Literature in Education,* Mar. 2003, *34*(1), 47–55; Margaret and Michael Rustin, "Where Is Home? An Essay on Philip Pullman's *Northern Lights,*" *Journal of Child Psychotherapy,* 2003, *29,* 93–105; Margaret and Michael Rustin, "A New Kind of Friendship—An Essay on Philip Pullman's *The Subtle Knife,*" *Journal of Child Psychotherapy,* 2003, *29,* 227–241; Margaret and Michael Rustin, "Learning to Say Goodbye: An Essay on Philip Pullman's *The Amber Spyglass,*" *Journal of Child Psychotherapy,* 2003, *29*(3), 415–428; Naomi Wood, "Paradise Lost and Found: Obedience, Disobedience, and Storytelling in C. S. Lewis and Philip Pullman," *Children's Literature in Education,* Dec. 2001, *32*(4), 237–259.

12. Anonymous, "About the Writing," Philip Pullman's Author Web site: http://www.philip-pullman .com/about_the_writing.asp (accessed Feb. 19, 2007).

13. Steve Meacham, "The Shed Where God Died," *The Sidney Morning Herald,* Dec. 13, 2003; available at

http://www.smh.com.au/articles/2003/12/12/107112
5644900.html?from=storyrhs (accessed Jan. 1, 2007).

14. See Michael Burleigh's *Earthy Powers: The Clash of Religion and Politics in Europe from the French Revolution to the Great War* (New York: HarperCollins, 2006).

15. For more information about the films, please see the following Web site for *The Golden Compass:* http://www.goldencompassmovie.com/ (accessed Feb. 19, 2007).

16. Philip Pullman, "The Darkside of Narnia," *The Guardian,* Oct. 1, 1998, 6–7.

17. Philip Pullman, Carnegie Medal Acceptance Speech, partial transcript, available at http://www.random house.com/features/pullman/author/carnegie.html (accessed Jan. 1, 2007).

18. Laura Miller, "Far from Narnia: Philip Pullman's Secular Fantasy for Children," *The New Yorker,* Dec. 26, 2005; available at http://www.newyorker.com/fact/content /articles/051226fa_fact (accessed June 18, 2006).

19. Celia Dodd, "Debate: Human Nature: Universally Acknowledged," *The Times,* May 8, 2004; available at http://www.timesonline.co.uk/printFriendly /0,,1-100-1100513,00.html (accessed June 19, 2006).

20. Kate Kellaway, "A Wizard with Worlds," *The Observer,* Oct. 22, 2000; available at http://observer.guardian .co.uk/review/story/0,6903,638058,00.html (accessed Dec. 31, 2006).

21. Laura Miller, "Far from Narnia."

22. Laura Miller, "Far from Narnia."

23. Susan Roberts, "A Dark Agenda," Surefish.co.uk (Nov.

2002); available at http://www.surefish.co.uk/culture/
features/pullman_interview.htm (accessed June 19,
2006).

24. Caroline Haydon, "Why Philip Pullman Wants to Teach
Children About Atheism," *The Independent,* Mar. 2, 2006;
available at http://education.independent.co.uk
/schools/article348592.ece (accessed June 19, 2006).

25. The full quote from Pullman is as follows: "Imagine
this: every night for a year . . . there's a very short
straight-to-camera piece—no longer than five minutes—
in which a different person each day speaks about a
book they love. No competition; no voting; no distract-
ing visuals; no ranking in order; literary people and
non-literary people, old books and new books, fiction,
poetry, biography—anything. Just the face of a human
being talking about a book they admire passionately, in
a wide democracy of reading. It would be the best thing
on television" (Philip Pullman, "The Big Read," *The
Times,* Dec. 20, 2003); reprinted on Philip Pullman's
Author Web site, http://www.philip-pullman.com/pages
/content/index.asp?PageID=98 (accessed June 16, 2006).

26. He has even written on the Republic of Heaven—a kind
of utopia-without-God on earth, the building of which
occupies most of *The Amber Spyglass,* as if it were to be
built now, in our own world. See Philip Pullman, "The
Republic of Heaven," *The Horn Book Magazine,* Nov./Dec.
2001, 655–667.

27. Daniel P. Moloney, "An Almost Christian Fantasy," *First
Things,* May 2001, *113,* 48. For an almost identical
review, see Andrew Stuttaford, "Sunday School for Athe-

ists," *National Review,* Mar. 25, 2002, 56–58, especially p. 57: "For he [Pullman] is, alas, a man with a message, and by the end of the trilogy the message has drowned out the magic. Narrative thrust is abandoned in favor of a hectoring, pontificating peachiness. . . . Pullman, you see, is a man with an apse to grind. He hates the Church, and he hates it with a passion." *Anti-Catholics in Controversies — Keating*

28. Even Tony Watkins's wonderful book about the trilogy, though it takes issue with Pullman's atheism as a conflict for religious believers, does not go far in disputing whether the trilogy actually is atheistic in nature. Pullman's word seems to be the last word on this matter.

29. This "Death of God" group included Thomas J. J. Altizer of Emory University, William Hamilton of Colgate Rochester Divinity School, and Paul Van Buren of Temple University. See "Toward a Hidden God," *Time,* Apr. 8, 1966; available at http://www.time.com/time /magazine/printout/0,8816,835309,00.html (accessed Dec. 29, 2006).

30. *Time* reprinted this obituary in its "Is God Dead?" issue. The obituary had appeared as satire in a Methodist student magazine at the time.

31. Umberto Eco asserts that all artists, writers included, offer us in their creations "works in movement": "In other words, the author offers the interpreter, the performer, the addressee a work to be completed. He does not know the exact fashion in which his work will be concluded, but he is aware that once completed the work in question will still be his own. It will not be a different work, and, at the end of the interpretative

dialogue, a form which is his form will have been organized, even though it may have been assembled by an outside party in a particular way that he could not have foreseen. . . . Every work of art, even though it is produced by following an explicit or implicit poetics of necessity, is effectively open to a virtually unlimited range of possible readings, each of which causes the work to acquire new vitality in terms of one particular taste, or perspective, or personal performance" (Eco, *The Open Work,* 19–21).

32. Philip Pullman, "Voluntary Service" available at http://books.guardian.co.uk/review/story/0,120848655 61,00html (accessed Apr. 27, 2007).

Part One

1. Frederich Nietzsche, *Thus Spoke Zarathustra: A Book for None and All,* trans. Walter Kauman. New York: Penguin, 1978, 12.

2. Sandra Schneiders, *Women and the Word.* Mahwah, N.J.: Paulist Press, 1986, 8–19.

3. Dorothee Söelle, *To Work and to Love: A Theology of Creation.* Philadelphia: Fortress Press, 1984, 129–156.

4. See Luce Irigaray's "La Mystérique," *Speculum of the Other Woman,* trans. Gillian C. Gill (Ithaca, N.Y.: Cornell University Press, 1985, 191–202); Grace Jantzen's *Becoming Divine: Toward a Feminist Philosophy of Religion* (Bloomington, Ind.: Indiana University Press, 1999, 40–53).

Chapter One

1. Carol Christ, *She Who Changes: Re-Imagining the Divine in the World.* New York: Palgrave MacMillan, 2003, 25.

2. Pullman explained to *New Yorker* writer Laura Miller that "all of the imaginative sympathy of [*Paradise Lost*] is with Satan rather than with God" (Miller, "Far from Narnia").

3. Sallie McFague, *Models of God.* Philadelphia: Fortress Press, 1987, 65.

4. G.W.F. Hegel, *Phenomenology of Spirit,* trans. A. V. Miller. New York: Oxford University Press, 1979, 541.

5. FrederichNietzsche, *Thus Spoke Zarathustra: A Book for None and All,* trans. Walter Kauman. New York: Penguin, 1978, 261.

6. Peter Hitchens, "This Is the Most Dangerous Author in Britain," originally published in *The Daily Mail,* Jan. 27, 2002, p. 63; available at http://home.wlv.ac.uk /~bu1895/hitchens.htm (accessed June 30, 2006).

7. Nietzsche, *Thus Spoke Zarathustra,* 41.

8. Gianni Vattimo, *Dialogue with Nietzsche,* trans. William McCuaig. New York: Columbia University Press, 2000, 91–95.

9. Nietzsche, *Thus Spoke Zarathustra,* 297.

10. Please see the following related resources: Alfred North Whitehead's *Process and Reality* (New York: Free Press, 1979); Gustavo Gutiérrez's *A Theology of Liberation* (Maryknoll, N.Y.: Orbis Books, 1990); Jon Sobrino's *Spirituality of Liberation: Toward Political Holiness* (Maryknoll, N.Y.: Orbis Books, 1989); Sallie McFague's *Metaphorical Theology: Models of God in Religious Language* (Philadelphia: Fortress Press, 1982); Catherine Keller's *The Face of the Deep* (New York: Routledge, 2003).

11. See, for example, Elie Wiesel, *The Trial of God* (New York: Random House, 1979) or Fyodor Dostoevsky, *The*

Brothers Karamazov, trans. Richard Pevear (Farrar, Straus, & Giroux, 2002), Book V, chapter 4.

12. See I-Hsuan, *The Zen Teachings of Master Lin-Chi,* trans. Burton Watson (New York: Columbia University Press, 1999, 52).

13. For the quote and this characterization, see James Livingston's *Anatomy of the Sacred: An Introduction to Religion,* 4th ed. (Upper Saddle River, N.J.: Prentice Hall, 2001, 243–244).

Chapter Two

1. Lao Tzu, Tao Te Ching, #56. trans. Jane English. New York: Vintage Books, 1997.

2. See chapters 7 and 8 of Elisabeth Johnson's *She Who Is: The Mystery of God in Feminist Theological Discourse* (New York: Herder & Herder, 1993, 124–169).

3. For a full treatment of the Wisdom Sophia, see Elizabeth Johnson's *She Who Is.*

4. Grace Jantzen, *Becoming Divine: Toward a Feminist Philosophy of Religion.* Bloomington: Indiana University Press, 1999, 255.

5. Reference to "pandemonium" appears many times in *Paradise Lost,* including the very first section of Book I. Please see, *John Milton's Paradise Lost,* David Hawkes, ed. (New York: Barnes & Noble Classics, 2004, 10).

6. Carol Christ, *She Who Changes: Re-Imagining the Divine in the World.* New York: Palgrave MacMillan, 2003, 209.

7. See, for example, Alfred North Whitehead, *Process and Reality* (New York: Free Press, 1979).

8. Grace Jantzen is one such example of a liberation theologian with panentheistic views of God (though most

regard her as more of a philosopher of religion, we see her as a kind of feminist theologian), as is Dorothee Söelle, who is explicit about her stance as a liberation theologian and panentheistic vision of the divine throughout her work.

9. See David Tracy, *Blessed Rage for Order* (Chicago: University of Chicago Press, 1996).

10. Pierre Teilhard de Chardin, *The Divine Milieu*. New York: Harper Perennial Modern Classics, 2001.

11. Carol Christ, *She Who Changes*, 205.

12. Carol Christ, *She Who Changes*, 208.

13. Carol Christ, *She Who Changes*, 209.

Chapter Three

1. Kim Campbell, "Looking Through His Dark Material for Light: An Interview with Philip Pullman," *Christian Science Monitor*, 2001, 93(57), 16.

2. Eric Warmington and Philip Rouse, "Pheado," in *The Great Dialogues of Plato*, trans. W.H.D. Rouse. New York: New American Library, 1984, 480–484.

3. See Aristotle's *De Anima* (On the Soul).

4. Sources for this belief include the biblical testimony to it in a variety of places: Ezekiel's vision of the resurrected bones turning back into bodies (Ezekiel 37:1–11), St. Paul's discussion of the resurrected body (1 Corinthians 15:36–45), and Jesus' own resurrected existence (for example, Luke 24:36–49). For the Catholic Church, also see *The Catechism of the Catholic Church*, paragraph 1016.

5. The earliest compilation of gnostic texts was St. Irenaeus's *Adversus Haereses* (*Against Heresies*), written

between 175–185 A.D. He outlines the varieties of gnostic beliefs and quotes heavily from their written works. For a contemporary collection of ancient gnostic texts, see Marvin Meyer's *The Gnostic Gospels of Jesus* (San Francisco: HarperSanFrancisco, 2005).

6. This passage is from chapter 2 of the Bhagavad-Gita, which is part of the larger Hindu epic, the Mahabharata.

7. For a history of thought and teaching on the trinity, see Catherine LaCugna's *God for Us: The Trinity and Christian Life* (San Francisco: HarperSanFrancisco, 1993).

8. See Grace Jantzen's work as one example of this particular viewpoint, as discussed in Chapter Two, and Sallie McFague as another, as discussed in Part Three.

9. For the quote, see Andrew Stuttaford, "Sunday School for Atheists," *National Review,* Mar. 25, 2002, 57.

Part Two

1. This understanding of the good that Pullman presupposes in his trilogy is an Aristotelian notion of the good appropriated and expanded by the Christian tradition, most notably by Thomas Aquinas. It is not the only tradition. Emotivism, often represented by David Hume in his *An Inquiry Concerning the Principles of Morals,* argued that the good is what feels good (pleasure) and the bad is what feels bad (pain). Utilitarians (see John Stuart Mill's *Utilitarianism* for a good example) built on the emotivists by adding that people's actions should be directed by the principle that greatest good for the greatest number should be done. Formalism, usually associated with Immanuel Kant in his *Groundwork of the*

Metaphysics of Morals, defines good as that which meets certain formal rules. For example, Kant's rule was "Always act according to that maxim whose universality as a law you can at the same time will." Finally, relativism defines the good as dependent on individual, social, or cultural preferences. As with so many of the ideas implicit in the trilogy, Pullman's ethics is built on a classical Christian foundation.

2. For a recognition that Pullman's ethics is found implicitly in the words and actions of the characters, see Naomi Wood, "Paradise Lost and Found: Obedience, Disobedience, and Storytelling in C. S. Lewis and Philip Pullman." In *Children's Literature in Education,* Dec. 2001, *32*(4), 237–259, especially p. 244.

Chapter Four

1. Karl Marx's quote on religion being the "opium of the people" is found in the preface to his 1843 *Contribution to the Critique of Hegel's Philosophy of Right.* The idea behind this statement—that one should measure words by their usage—is an idea that Marx developed from Ludwig Feuerbach, who used it in his critique of Christianity in his *The Essence of Christianity.* Two major schools of ethical theory have expanded on Marx's idea. Analytical philosophy—the first school—analyzes language itself as a way to understand the world. Ludwig Wittgenstein's *Philosophical Investigations* is a good representative. Postmodern philosophy—the second school— explores how social and personal histories create the meaning of the words we use. A good example of this approach is Frederick Nietzsche's *The Genealogy of*

Morals. Gustavo Gutierrez's *A Theology of Liberation* was a seminal work in bringing this type of analysis into mainstream theology.

2. Dorothee Söelle, *Christ the Representative: Essays in Theology After the "Death of God,"* trans. David Lewis. Philadelphia: Fortress Press, 1967, 9.

3. Gustavo Guitérrez, *A Theology of Liberation.*Maryknoll, N.Y.: Orbis Books, 1990.

4. Letty Russell, *Human Liberation in a Feminist Perspective.* Philadelphia: Westminster Press, 1974, 93.

5. This understanding of evil—that it parades as good—is similar to the classical Christian definition of evil as the privation of some good. Augustine was one of the first Christians to articulate this view (see his *Enchiridion of Faith, Hope, and Love*); because of his influence in Western Christian thought, this view tended to dominate theology well into the twentieth century. Contemporary challenges have been raised against it, most notably that this definition seems to imply that the evil of an event like the Holocaust is just the "absence of good"—an understanding that appears wholly inadequate, given what occurred. For these criticisms and alternative views of evil, see Lucien Richard, *What Are They Saying About the Theology of Suffering?* (New York: Paulist Press, 1993).

6. This definition of the prophet comes from *The Catholic Study Bible,* 2nd ed. (New York: Oxford University Press, 2006) that defines the prophet (p. 1704) as "called by God to speak the truth no matter what the cost" and "did not specialize in predicting the future but analyzing the present and announcing the consequences of current behavior." This definition, found in the glos-

sary, is a standard one with Biblical scholars. It is not the standard definition for fundamentalists, who tend to define the prophet as one who predicts the future. We prefer the first definition, as it takes seriously the historical setting of the prophetic writings, their content, and the role of human beings in their composition.

7. See, for example, chapter 5 of Elisabeth Schussler Fiorenza's *Jesus: Miriam's Child, Sophia's Prophet* (New York: Continuum International Publishing, 1994) and chapter 6 of Jon Sobrino's *Jesus the Liberator* (Maryknoll, N.Y.: Orbis Press, 1994).

Chapter Five

1. John Henry Newman, *An Essay on the Development of Christian Doctrine,* 6th ed. South Bend, Ind.: University of Notre Dame Press, 1989, 40.

2. Thomas Aquinas, *Summa Contra Gentiles,* Book 1, chapter 36. Defining "human nature" has come under extensive controversy lately. Aristotle believed that human nature—what distinguished human beings from other species—was its capacity for higher reasoning. This idea gets appropriated by most of Western Christian thought, including Augustine and Aquinas. The major criticism of this notion of nature is that it is (1) static and thus does not account for human evolution and development, and (2) that it is thoroughly Western and thus often masks a philosophical colonialism (that is, dismissing thoughts from other cultures that do not make these seem presumptions about human nature). Responses to these criticisms have been varied. Ralph McInerny in his *Ethica Thomistica* (Washington, D.C.: Catholic University of America, 1997) argues that

"reasoning" was the human capacity to organize all sorts of activities in an intelligent manner. Hence, human nature was not the static ability to make logical deductions but the dynamic capacity to organize life. Alasdair MacIntyre argued in *After Virtue* (Notre Dame, Ind.: University of Notre Dame Press, 1984) that that nature should be understood in the context of a historically unfolding intellectual and social tradition. Hence, neither nature nor thought about nature is static. It grows and changes through history. Finally, Elisabeth Johnson in her *Consider Jesus* (New York: Herder & Herder, 1992) redefines human nature, not as reason but as being to relate to other human beings.

3. John Rowe Townsend, "Paradise Reshaped," *The Horn Book Magazine*, July/Aug. 2002, 419.

4. See Dietrich Bonhoeffer's *Letters and Papers from Prison* (New York: Touchstone, 1987).

5. Michael Himes, *Doing the Truth in Love: Conversations about God, Relationship, and Service.* New York: Paulist Press, 1995.

Chapter Six

1. Pullman quipped this during his Carnegie Medal acceptance speech in 1996.

2. Dead Man Walking Updates, "Updates to Key Facts and Figures Cited in Dead Man Walking"; available at http://www.deadmanwalkingupdate.org/dmw_stats .html (accessed Jan. 2, 2007).

3. This quote is a theme running through Dorothy Day's *The Long Loneliness* (San Francisco: HarperSanFrancisco, 1997).

4. These two different types of freedom have been part of Western thought since the ancient Greeks. Recently,

however, the notion of freedom "from" has come to dominate contemporary thought. For an analysis of these two notions and the rise of freedom "from" in Catholic Christian thought, see Servais Pinckaers' *The Sources of Christian Ethics,* trans. Mary Thomas Noble (Washington, D.C.: Catholic University of America Press, 1995).

Part Three

1. Daniel P. Moloney, "An Almost Christian Fantasy," *First Things,* May 2001, *113,* 45–49.

Chapter Seven

1. Letter to Dutch physicist Heike Kamerlingh-Onne's widow, Feb. 25, 1926; Einstein Archive 14-389.
2. Carol Christ, *She Who Changes: Re-Imagining the Divine in the World.* New York: Palgrave MacMillan, 2003, 207. Christ is quoting Valerie Saiving.
3. Dorothee Söelle, *To Work and to Love: A Theology of Creation* (Philadelphia: Fortress Press, 1984, 7).
4. Dorothee Söelle, *To Work and to Love,* 8.
5. Dorothee Söelle, *To Work and to Love,* 10.

Chapter Eight

1. Alfred Lord Tennyson, "Fatima," in *Poetical Works* (Ware Hertfordshire: Wordsworth Edition Limited, 1994).
2. Christians have historically had an ambivalent attitude toward *eros.* The early Christians adopted many ideas from the broader culture but tended to distrust *eros,* as it overpowered reason and caused one to lose control. Up through the late medieval period, *eros* was viewed as a kind of madness that clouded one's judgment and,

given its fleeting nature, was a poor foundation for marriage. It is not until the late twentieth century that Christians become more comfortable speaking about physical love as good and important for the spiritual life. Nowhere is this more prominent that in John Paul II's *Theology of the Body* (Boston: Pauline Books and Media, 1997). The late pope's perspective was affirmed by his successor, Pope Benedict XVI, in his first encyclical *Deus Caritas Est.*

3. For a psychological perspective on Lyra and Will's dependence on "surrogate parental figures" see again Margaret and Michael Rustin, "Where Is Home? An Essay on Philip Pullman's Northern Lights," *Journal of Child Psychotherapy,* 2003, *29*(1), 93–105.

4. For a psychological perspective on Lyra and Will's growing friendship, see again Margaret and Michael Rustin, "A New Kind of Friendship: An Essay on Philip Pullman's *The Subtle Knife,*" *Journal of Child Psychotherapy,* 2003, *29*(2), 227–241.

5. Dorothee Söelle, *To Work and to Love: A Theology of Creation.* Philadelphia: Fortress Press, 1984, 136.

6. One of Pullman's major criticism of C. S. Lewis and J.R.R. Tolkien is that Pullman believes these authors neglect this physical aspect of life. See Pullman's "The Republic of Heaven," *The Horn Book Magazine,* Nov./Dec. 2001, 655–667, particularly p. 661.

7. It should be noted that the reading offered here of Genesis as a story of the fall and original sin is a distinctively Christian one. Christians read Genesis through Paul's Letter to the Romans, chapter 5. Jews, who share this same story with Christians, do not read it in this fashion at all. They do not see the story as one about

the fall of humanity but one about a couple and their relationship with God.

8. This was the affirmation of the Council of Chalcedon in 451 that Jesus was fully human and that his assumption of a human body meant that humans were saved, body and soul. The belief that Christians are anti-body stems from a persistent interpretation of asceticism (from both Christians and non-Christians) as a hatred of the body instead of ordering of the body and soul to their proper goods.

9. Sallie McFague, *Models of God*. Philadelphia: Fortress Press, 1987, 130.

10. McFague, *Models of God*, 131.

11. McFague, *Models of God*.

12. Dorothee Söelle, *To Work and to Love*, 134.

13. Dorothee Söelle, *To Work and to Love*, 134.

14. McFague, *Models of God*, 135.

Chapter Nine

1. For the Catholic Church's understanding of Mary see The Catechism of the Catholic Church, paragraphs 487–507; available at http://www.vatican.va/archive/ENG0015/__P1K.HTM (accessed Jan. 1, 2007).

2. Sallie McFague, *Models of God*. Philadelphia: Fortress Press, 1987, 135.

3. For a psychological perspective on Lyra and Will's decision to separate, see Margaret and Michael Rustin, "Learning to Say Goodbye: An Essay on Philip Pullman's *The Amber Spyglass*," *Journal of Child Psychotherapy*, 2003, *29*(3), 415–428.

4. In reflecting on Jesus, contemporary theology distinguishes two different approaches. The first is a

top-down approach. It begins with Jesus' divinity and studies how this is expressed in the actions of Jesus' life. This has been the approach for most of Christian history. See St. Anselm's *Why Did God Become Man?* as a classical representative of this approach. The second approach is a bottom-up approach. It begins with Jesus' humanity, tries to understand his life in human terms first and foremost, and relates the divinity to this humanity. Although some of these approaches have denied Jesus' divinity, others have insisted that they are merely following St. Paul's line of thought in the third chapter of his letter to the Philippians, where Jesus though "he was in the form of God . . . he emptied himself . . . coming in human likeness." A good example of this latter approach is John Meier, *A Marginal Jew* (New York: Doubleday, 1991).

5. See "Poems in Stanzas," from *Hadewijch: The Complete Works,* trans. Mother Columba Hart, O.S.B. (New York: Paulist Press, 1980, 123–258).

Conclusion

1. Pullman echoes almost these exact same values in his "The Republic of Heaven," *The Horn Book Magazine* (Nov./Dec. 2001) on pages 666–667: "dishonesty is bad and truthfulness is good, selfishness is wrong and generosity is right," "trying to restrict understanding and put knowledge in chains is bad," "live by the imagination," "the common place belongs to everyone," "be cheerful," "good will is . . . a moral imperative," and "we provide for ourselves."

2. See Victor E. Frankl's *Man's Search for Meaning* (New York: Rider & Co., 2004).

ABOUT THE AUTHORS

Donna Freitas is assistant professor of religion at Boston University. Donna loves to ask Big Questions (Why *are* we here anyway?) and delights in discovering the many possible forums in which to dabble with the stuff of faith, religion, spirituality, literature, and gender. A regular contributor to *Beliefnet* and *Publishers Weekly*, she has also written for *The Wall Street Journal*, *The Washington Post*, *Christian Century*, and *School Library Journal*; she has appeared as a commentator on NPR's *All Things Considered*. Her books include *Becoming a Goddess of Inner Poise: Spirituality for the Bridget Jones in All of Us*, and *Save the Date: A Spirituality of Dating, Love, Dinner & the Divine*, which she cowrote with her friend Jason King. She looks forward to the publication of her first novel, *The Possibilities of Sainthood*, with Farrar, Straus, & Giroux, in 2008. Born in Rhode Island, Donna now divides her time between New York City and Boston. She can be contacted directly through her Web site at www.donnafreitas.com.

Jason King graduated from Berea College in Kentucky, where he played soccer, ran track, worked in the computer center, majored in math and philosophy, and read countless fantasy and sci-fi novels. After college, he taught elementary school for a year in Chicago, after which he realized he wanted to teach college. He went to Washington, D.C., and pursued his Ph.D. in theology, ethics, and culture from the Catholic

University of America. There he had many conversations with his friends, including his future wife, about the merits of fantasy literature for the study of theology. He is assistant professor of theology at Saint Vincent College in Latrobe, Pennsylvania, and continues to love his interactions with students and colleagues. He now has two children to whom he daily reads "once upon a times."

INDEX

Other Books of Interest

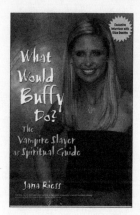

What Would Buffy Do?
The Vampire Slayer as Spiritual Guide
Jana Riess
Paper
ISBN: 978-0-7879-6922-6

"...muses upon the religious themes in the television series." (*Publishers Weekly,* February 9, 2004)

"A major contribution to our understanding of Buffy and twenty-first century spirituality. *What Would Buffy Do?* may be the best brief introduction to all aspects of this amazing television series."

—David Lavery, coeditor, *Slayage: The Online International Journal of Buffy Studies*

"Jana Riess brilliantly articulates how the Slayer's battle against evil celebrates the core spiritual values held dear by people of faith. Rock it, Sister Riess!"

—Nancy Holder, author; *BTVS: The Watcher's Guide, Volume 1; The Evil That Men Do;* and *Immortal*

Finally, a book that explores some of the show's most fascinating spiritual, religious, and mythological ideas, from apocalypse and iconography to the power of blood and the need for humor in fighting our spiritual battles.

Jana Riess is currently the Religion Book Review editor for *Publishers Weekly* and is also the author of *The Spiritual Traveler: Boston and New England.* She has written for *Books & Culture,* Beliefnet .com, and *Kirkus* and received a Ph.D in American religious history from Columbia University. She is a recognized expert on trends in American religion and publishing and is often interviewed by local and national media.

Christian Wisdom of the Jedi Masters
Dick Staub
Cloth
ISBN: 978-0-7879-7894-5

"Dick Staub's tour through the spirituality of *Star Wars* is inspiring and fun. Anyone, like me, who grew up lionizing Luke Skywalker and Princess Leia should read this book. It will both carry you back to your childhood and support your spirit as you make your way through adulthood."
—Lauren Winner, author, *Girl Meets God* and *Real Sex: The Naked Truth about Chastity*

"For years Dick Staub has been digging into popular culture to expose the threads of spiritual gold that run through it. *Star Wars* is his mother lode, and with eloquence he echoes Master Yoda announcing to young seekers, 'Already know you that which you need.'"
—Jeffrey Overstreet, film columnist/critic, *Christianity Today* and *Paste Magazine*

"Like a Jedi master, Dick Staub delivers sharp, counter-intuitive insights that the next generation seeks. Prepare to discover a force far greater than any you ever imagined."
—Craig Detweiler, author, *A Matrix of Meanings: Finding God in Pop Culture*

Written by award-winning radio personality Dick Staub, this compelling book is filled with anecdotes from the *Star Wars* films that serve as a launching pad into rediscovering authentic Christianity. *Christian Wisdom of the Jedi Masters* also contains quotes from revered "Jedi Christians" such as Thomas Merton, Teresa of Avila, the Apostle Paul, G. K. Chesterton, and other theologians, mystics, writers, and philosophers. The author sheds new light on the struggles and challenges of living faithfully in postmodern life and offers a reintroduction to what C. S. Lewis and J. R. R. Tolkien called the "one true myth," Christianity.

Into the Wardrobe
C. S. Lewis and the Narnia Chronicles
David C. Downing
Cloth
ISBN: 978-0-7879-7890-7

"What David C. Downing does so well is give us lenses through which Lewis's myriad works come into sharp focus, revealing the convictions, insights, scholarship, experience, and questions that shaped the man who brought us Narnia."

—Jeffrey Overstreet, film critic,
Christianity Today and LookingCloser.org

"Like his previous studies of Lewis's life and writings, *Into the Wardrobe* proves again that Downing is a master at weaving essential facts and fresh insights into a smooth narrative—a balanced and satisfying guide for either experienced or first-time readers of Narnia."

—Robert Trexler, editor,
CSL: The Bulletin of the New York C. S. Lewis Society

Published in the early 1950s, C. S. Lewis's seven Chronicles of Narnia were proclaimed instant children's classics and have been hailed in *The Oxford Companion to Children's Literature* as "the most sustained achievement in fantasy for children by a twentieth-century author." But how could Lewis (a formidable critic, scholar, and Christian apologist) conjure up the kind of adventures in which generations of children (and adults) take such delight? In this engaging and insightful book, C. S. Lewis expert David C. Downing invites readers to join his vivid exploration of the Chronicles of Narnia, offering a detailed look at the enchanting stories themselves as well as focusing on the extraordinary intellect and imagination of the man behind the Wardrobe.

David C. Downing is a leading C. S. Lewis expert and an award-winning author. His articles about Lewis have appeared in such publications as *Christianity Today, Christianity and Literature, Books & Culture, Christian Scholars Review*, and numerous other journals.